EXAMINING THE ADMINISTRATION'S TREATMENT OF WHISTLEBLOWERS

HEARING

BEFORE THE

SUBCOMMITTEE ON FEDERAL WORKFORCE, US POSTAL SERVICE AND THE CENSUS

OF THE

COMMITTEE ON OVERSIGHT AND GOVERNMENT REFORM

HOUSE OF REPRESENTATIVES

ONE HUNDRED THIRTEENTH CONGRESS

SECOND SESSION

SEPTEMBER 9, 2014

Serial No. 113–139

Printed for the use of the Committee on Oversight and Government Reform

Available via the World Wide Web: http://www.fdsys.gov
http://www.house.gov/reform

U.S. GOVERNMENT PRINTING OFFICE

89–898 PDF   WASHINGTON : 2014

For sale by the Superintendent of Documents, U.S. Government Printing Office
Internet: bookstore.gpo.gov   Phone: toll free (866) 512–1800; DC area (202) 512–1800
Fax: (202) 512–2104   Mail: Stop IDCC, Washington, DC 20402–0001

COMMITTEE ON OVERSIGHT AND GOVERNMENT REFORM

DARRELL E. ISSA, California, *Chairman*

JOHN L. MICA, Florida
MICHAEL R. TURNER, Ohio
JOHN J. DUNCAN, JR., Tennessee
PATRICK T. McHENRY, North Carolina
JIM JORDAN, Ohio
JASON CHAFFETZ, Utah
TIM WALBERG, Michigan
JAMES LANKFORD, Oklahoma
JUSTIN AMASH, Michigan
PAUL A. GOSAR, Arizona
PATRICK MEEHAN, Pennsylvania
SCOTT DesJARLAIS, Tennessee
TREY GOWDY, South Carolina
BLAKE FARENTHOLD, Texas
DOC HASTINGS, Washington
CYNTHIA M. LUMMIS, Wyoming
ROB WOODALL, Georgia
THOMAS MASSIE, Kentucky
DOUG COLLINS, Georgia
MARK MEADOWS, North Carolina
KERRY L. BENTIVOLIO, Michigan
RON DeSANTIS, Florida

ELIJAH E. CUMMINGS, Maryland, *Ranking Minority Member*
CAROLYN B. MALONEY, New York
ELEANOR HOLMES NORTON, District of Columbia
JOHN F. TIERNEY, Massachusetts
WM. LACY CLAY, Missouri
STEPHEN F. LYNCH, Massachusetts
JIM COOPER, Tennessee
GERALD E. CONNOLLY, Virginia
JACKIE SPEIER, California
MATTHEW A. CARTWRIGHT, Pennsylvania
TAMMY DUCKWORTH, Illinois
ROBIN L. KELLY, Illinois
DANNY K. DAVIS, Illinois
TONY CARDENAS, California
STEVEN A. HORSFORD, Nevada
MICHELLE LUJAN GRISHAM, New Mexico
Vacancy

LAWRENCE J. BRADY, *Staff Director*
JOHN D. CUADERES, *Deputy Staff Director*
STEPHEN CASTOR, *General Counsel*
LINDA A. GOOD, *Chief Clerk*
DAVID RAPALLO, *Minority Staff Director*

SUBCOMMITTEE ON FEDERAL WORKFORCE, U.S. POSTAL SERVICE AND THE CENSUS

BLAKE FARENTHOLD, Texas, *Chairman*

TIM WALBERG, Michigan
TREY GOWDY, South Carolina
DOUG COLLINS, Georgia
RON DeSANTIS, Florida

STEPHEN F. LYNCH, Massachusetts, *Ranking Minority Member*
ELEANOR HOLMES NORTON, District of Columbia
WM. LACY CLAY, Missouri

CONTENTS

EXAMINING THE ADMINISTRATION'S TREATMENT OF WHISTLEBLOWERS

Tuesday, September 9, 2014

House of Representatives,
Subcommittee on Federal Workforce, U.S. Postal
Service, and the Census,
Committee on Oversight and Government Reform,
Washington, D.C.

The subcommittee met, pursuant to call, at 2:00 p.m., in Room 2154, Rayburn House Office Building, Hon. Blake Farenthold [chairman of the subcommittee] presiding.

Present: Representatives Farenthold, Issa, Walberg, Lynch, Cummings, and Norton.

Staff Present: Melissa Beaumont, Assistant Clerk; Will L. Boyington, Deputy Press Secretary; Molly Boyl, Deputy General Counsel and Parliamentarian; Linda Good, Chief Clerk; James Robertson, Senior Professional Staff Member; Jessica Seale, Digital Director; Andrew Shult, Deputy Digital Director; Peter Warren, Legislative Policy Director; Jaron Bourke, Minority Administrative Director; Krista Boyd, Minority Deputy Director of Legislation/ Counsel; Lena Chang, Minority Counsel; Courtney Cochran, Minority Press Secretary; Tim Lynch, Minority Counsel; Mark Stephenson, Minority Director of Legislation; and Michael Wilkins, Minority Staff Assistant.

Mr. FARENTHOLD. Good afternoon. The Subcommittee on the Federal Workforce, U.S. Postal Service and the Census will come to order. I'd like to begin this hearing by stating the Oversight Committee mission statement. We exist to secure two fundamental principles. First, Americans have a right to know the money Washington takes from them is well spent. And second, Americans deserve an efficient, effective government that works for them.

Our duty on the Oversight and Government Reform Committee is to protect these rights. Our solemn responsibility is to hold government accountable to taxpayers because taxpayers have a right to know what they get from their government. We will work tirelessly, in partnership with citizen watchdogs, to deliver the facts to the American people and bring genuine reform to the Federal bureaucracy. This is the mission of the Oversight and Government Reform Committee.

I'll now start with my opening statement. One of the most important functions of the Oversight Committee is to help expose waste, fraud, and abuse within the Federal bureaucracy, and to help reform broken institutions and policies that ensure taxpayers that they have a government that works for them. As members of this

(1)

committee know, whistleblowers are an invaluable asset in helping us achieve this important goal. Unfortunately, those who expose waste, fraud, and abuse from the inside sometimes only receive retaliation as their award.

Today's hearing will examine how whistleblower protection laws are often ignored or manipulated. The result is that those in a position to shine light on illegal behavior stay in the shadows for fear of retribution.

This committee has a long history of working with whistleblowers. They aid in our investigations, and we appropriately have legislative jurisdiction over laws that provide them protections.

In 2012, we updated the Whistleblower Protection Act to expand existing disclosure protections and to create new avenues for appellate review outside the Federal circuit, which has historically not been friendly to whistleblowers. I want to hear how the newest amendments to the law are working and whether or not the executive branch is violating either the letter or the spirit of the law.

I'm also pleased that two brave whistleblowers are with us today so we can hear firsthand accounts of the good, the bad, and ugly of doing the right thing and coming forward to report misdeeds in their own agency. I want to thank you all for your service, courage and willingness to speak today.

Congress must do everything in its power to help protect well-intentioned individuals who help Congress and the public know when improper behavior occurs within the Federal bureaucracy. Again, I would like to thank all the witnesses for participating today.

I now recognize the ranking member, the gentleman from Massachusetts, Mr. Lynch, for his opening statement.

Mr. LYNCH. Thank you, Mr. Chairman. I appreciate your holding this hearing to examine the treatment of whistleblowers.

I also thank our witnesses for being here today and helping the committee with its work, and I look forward to your testimony.

Federal whistleblowers serve a valuable role in identifying waste, fraud, and abuse across the Federal Government. In many cases, the diligent oversight efforts undertaken by these government watchdogs shine a light on government abuse and, as a result, we're better able to safeguard American lives and mitigate the waste of American taxpayer resources.

It is these brave men and women who informed the American people about the government's delay in delivering armored cars to Iraq and Afghanistan, to reduce combat casualties from improvised explosive devices. Federal whistleblowers have also detailed the cancellation of U.S. Air marshals from flight protection duties despite the existence of confirmed and continued threats of potential terrorist hijackings. These dedicated government employees also reported the diversion of research funds that were set aside to treat veterans with traumatic brain injuries.

For many of these whistleblowers, doing the right thing and disclosing violations of law and fraud, waste, and abuse comes at a high price. Many have been subjected to acts of retaliation, including the elimination of their job duties, reassignment to positions of no consequence, geographical locations, such as the relocation of their desks to basements or closets, misconduct investigations, suspensions, and termination.

Mr. MacLean and Dr. Van Boven will testify how much their lives and the lives of their families were disrupted as a result of their retaliation that they faced. Unfortunately, whistleblower retaliation has been a longstanding problem over multiple administrations.

Much has been accomplished to enhance whistleblower protections. Congress, with the support and commitment of President Obama, passed the bipartisan Whistleblower Protection Enhancement Act in 2012 after more than a decade of reform efforts. This act strengthened protections for Federal employees by closing judicially created loopholes and extended new protections for government scientists and certain Transportation Security Administration employees. The bill also created a 2-year pilot.

That same year, the administration also extended whistleblower protections to Intelligence Community employees through a presidential directive. Congress then followed through this year by codifying protections for national security employees in the Intelligence Authorization Act. Although Congress and the administration can provide protections and avenues for redress, we cannot legislate culture. That can only change by determined leadership, constant attention from Congress, strong employee representatives, and strong Federal employee unions and vocal advocates.

Despite the progress we've made, our work is not yet complete, and I look forward to hearing from our witnesses about how much further we need to go.

Thank you, Mr. Chairman. I yield back the balance of my time.

Mr. FARENTHOLD. Thank you, Mr. Lynch.

Mr. FARENTHOLD. Members will have 7 days to submit opening statements for the record.

Mr. FARENTHOLD. We will now recognize our panel. The Honorable Carolyn Lerner is the head of the U.S. Office of Special Counsel. The Honorable Susan Tsui Grundmann is the Chairman of the U.S. Merit Systems Protection Board. Mr. Robert MacLean is a former employee of the U.S. Transportation Security Administration. Dr. Robert Van Boven is a former employee at the U.S. Department of Veterans Affairs. And Mr. Tom Devine is the legal director at the Government Accountability Project.

Pursuant to committee rule, all witnesses will be sworn before they testify. Would you please stand and raise your right hand? Do you solemnly swear or affirm that the testimony you are about to give will be the truth, the whole truth, and nothing but the truth?

Let the record reflect that all witnesses answered in the affirmative. You may be seated now.

We want to hear your opening testimony, but we also want to have the opportunity to question you, so those of you who submitted written testimony, we have your written testimony in front of us and have hopefully read it. And so in order to allow for discussion, we would appreciate your summarizing and hitting the high points and limiting your remarks to as close to 5 minutes as possible.

You'll see a countdown time in front of you. Much like the traffic lights we're all familiar with, green means go, yellow means speed up, and red means stop.

So we'll now start with Ms. Lerner. You're recognized for about 5 minutes.

WITNESS STATEMENTS

STATEMENT OF CAROLYN N. LERNER

Ms. LERNER. Thank you, Chairman Farenthold, Ranking Member Lynch, members of the committee. Thank you for inviting me to testify today about the Office of Special Counsel and its protection of Federal whistleblowers. In addition to protecting whistleblowers, we provide a safe channel for employees to disclose government wrongdoing. We enforce the Hatch Act, which keeps partisan politics out of the Federal workforce, and we protect returning servicemembers from unfair employment practices. We do all of this with a staff of about 120 and one of the smallest budgets of any law enforcement agency.

When I was appointed Special Counsel 3 years ago among my top goals was increasing awareness about and confidence in the agency. I believe we are succeeding on both fronts. This fiscal year we expect to receive over 5,000 cases for the first time in the agency's history, a 15 percent increase from last year and double the number of cases from 10 years ago.

Clearly, Federal employees now know who we are and feel confident coming to our agency, and we are getting great results on their behalf. In the past 2 years we've obtained 333 favorable actions for employees, about a 400 percent increase from 5 years ago, and we have done so while reducing the cost to resolve each case by over 40 percent.

With that introduction, I will now briefly discuss how we protect whistleblowers, the effect of the Whistleblower Protection Enhancement Act on OSC, and our education and outreach efforts.

When reviewing a whistleblower retaliation complaint, OSC's Complaints Examining Unit performs an initial review to determine if the complaint meets required elements. If it does, the matter is referred for further investigation. After we investigate, agencies often informally settle cases and take corrective actions. If an agency does not, we may then file a complaint with the MSPB, which can order the agency to do so.

Similarly, if an agency failed to take appropriate disciplinary action, we can file a complaint with the Board. OSC is able to protect complainants by seeking to delay or stay proposed adverse personnel actions, either informally with the agency or by filing a formal request with the MSPB. These stays provide temporary relief while OSC investigates.

Another tool that we use to get corrective actions is mediation. Very often, mediation resolves complaints to the mutual satisfaction of both agencies and complainants without the need for full investigation or litigation. For instance, in 2012, three employees of the Bureau of Alcohol, Tobacco and Firearms who blew the whistle on Operation Fast and Furious resolved their cases through OSC's mediation program.

The Whistleblower Protection Enhancement Act, which this committee worked hard to enact, has also strengthened OSC's ability to protect whistleblowers. The WPEA expanded OSC's jurisdiction, allowing us to take complaints that we previously would've had to dismiss due to narrow court interpretations of whistleblower protections.

The WPEA also improved OSC's ability to pursue disciplinary actions. For example, we recently filed complaints with the MSPB seeking disciplinary action against three Customs and Border Protection officials.

The WPEA also expanded OSC's authority to file amicus curiae briefs in cases related to Federal whistleblower retaliation. OSC has filed three amicus briefs in Federal courts, including one just this past month, and we are currently in discussions with the Department of Justice about OSC filing an amicus brief in the U.S. Supreme Court later this month in the MacLean v. Department of Homeland Security matter. This would follow the amicus brief that we filed in Mr. MacLean's case with the MSPB in August 2011.

These briefs are meant to help courts interpret the contours of whistleblower laws. We are optimistic that over time this will lead to a more pro-whistleblower body of juris prudence.

Finally, I want to very briefly address our education and outreach efforts and OSC's Certification Program. Government functions best and can address problems most effectively when employees can come forward without fear of retaliation. Creating this environment requires education, educating employees about their rights and managers about their responsibilities.

Accordingly, we have recently expanded our outreach and education efforts. In fiscal year 2014 we have conducted 90 training sessions throughout the Federal Government. This compares with 33 sessions just 3 years ago. We are also seeing an increase in the number of agencies seeking OSC's assistance in training employees on whistleblower laws. This positive increase is due in large part to the administration's recent requirement that agencies become certified through OSC's program.

I'd be happy to address this issue or any other in more detail in response to any of your questions. Thank you very much for the opportunity to testify today.

Mr. FARENTHOLD. Thank you very much, Ms. Lerner.

[Prepared statement of Ms. Lerner follows:]

Testimony of the Honorable Carolyn N. Lerner, Special Counsel
U.S. Office of Special Counsel

U.S. House of Representatives Committee on Oversight and Government Reform
Subcommittee on Federal Workforce, U.S. Postal Service and the Census

"Examining the Administration's Treatment of Whistleblowers"

September 9, 2014, 2:00 PM

Chairman Farenthold, Ranking Member Lynch, and Members of the Subcommittee:

Thank you for inviting me to testify today about the U.S. Office of Special Counsel (OSC) and its role in protecting whistleblowers in the federal government.

I. OSC's Role and Jurisdiction

OSC is an independent investigative and prosecutorial agency tasked with protecting the merit system and ensuring accountability and fairness for over 2.1 million civilian federal employees. Although my testimony today will focus primarily on OSC's role in investigating and prosecuting violations of prohibited personnel practices (PPPs) with respect to whistleblowers, we also enforce the merit system in several other ways. We serve as a safe and secure channel for federal employees to disclose government wrongdoing, specifically waste, fraud, abuse, mismanagement, and health and safety issues; we protect federal employees from all 13 PPPs, including reprisal for blowing the whistle, hiring offenses, and discrimination; we enforce the Hatch Act, which keeps partisan politics out of the federal workplace; and we support service members by enforcing the Uniformed Services Employment & Reemployment Rights Act (USERRA).

We serve the federal government and taxpayers with a staff of approximately 120 employees and one of the smallest budgets of any federal law enforcement agency. Still, even though we face the significant challenges of an ever-rising caseload, I am proud to say that we are more effective and efficient than ever before. By the close of fiscal year 2014, we expect to have received over 5,000 cases of all types for the first time in our agency's history, a 15 percent increase from last year and double the number of cases from ten years ago. This will include over 1,400 retaliation cases and over 1,500 whistleblower disclosures, an almost 30 percent increase from last year. In the past two years, we have obtained 333 favorable actions for federal employees, a threefold increase from five years ago. Importantly, we have achieved these results while at the same time reducing the cost to resolve each case by 41 percent over the past six years.

We receive cases from across the government. Our work often results in systemic changes that make government more efficient, cost effective, and safer for our citizens. Some recent examples are indicative of our work. In the past year, we addressed dozens of disclosures of fraud and waste in the payout of Administratively Uncontrollable Overtime at the Department of Homeland Security's (DHS) agencies. OSC's work with DHS whistleblowers has already resulted in changed practices that will save over $20 million a year. More recently, we have received hundreds of cases from Department of Veterans Affairs (VA) employees. These cases include disclosures of scheduling improprieties and threats to public health and safety, as well as complaints of whistleblower retaliation, which I will discuss later.

Finally, it is important to clarify that OSC's jurisdiction regarding whistleblower retaliation cases extends to many—but not all—current or former federal civilian employees or applicants for federal civilian employment. OSC does not, for example, have jurisdiction over active military personnel. Nor does OSC have jurisdiction over whistleblowers from intelligence agencies, such as the Federal Bureau of Investigation, the Central Intelligence Agency, or the National Security Agency. *See* 5 U.S.C. § 2302(a)(2)(C)(ii). However, on October 10, 2012, President Obama issued a Presidential Policy Directive that prohibits retaliation against whistleblowers in the Intelligence Community and requires intelligence agencies to establish a review process for claims of retaliation consistent with the procedures in the Whistleblower Protection Act (WPA).

With that introduction, I will discuss three main issues: (1) how we protect whistleblowers, (2) the effect of the Whistleblower Protection Enhancement Act of 2012 (WPEA) on our enforcement authority, and (3) our 2302(c) Certification Program and education and outreach efforts.

II.   How OSC Protects Whistleblowers

When a federal employee or applicant for federal employment believes they have faced reprisal for blowing the whistle, they have the option to file a complaint with OSC. When reviewing a whistleblower retaliation complaint, OSC analyzes the following four legal elements:

(1) did a protected disclosure of information occur;
(2) was a personnel action taken, not taken, or threatened;
(3) did those involved in the personnel action have actual or constructive knowledge of the protected disclosure; and
(4) was the protected disclosure a contributing factor in the personnel action.

If these four elements are met, the agency must show—by the high bar of clear and convincing evidence—that it would have taken the same action absent the whistleblower's disclosure. To assess this, we look at the strength of the agency's evidence in support of the personnel action, the existence and strength of the agency's motive to retaliate, and the treatment of similar agency employees who are not whistleblowers, as well as other factors.

If OSC's Complaints Examining Unit preliminarily determines that the complaint meets the four elements above, the matter is referred to our Investigation and Prosecution Division for further investigation. When appropriate, the complainant and the relevant agency may be given the option of mediation, which I will discuss in more detail below.

The law requires that OSC give the agency the opportunity to correct a prohibited personnel practice before we pursue a formal complaint. And as we investigate, agencies often do informally settle cases and take corrective action, restoring the *status quo ante*. These informal resolutions usually occur before OSC presents the case to the Merit Systems Protection Board (MSPB or Board), an administrative court in the executive branch that hears complaints regarding the federal merit system. But, if an agency does not take this opportunity, OSC may then file a complaint with the MSPB, which can order the agency to take corrective action.

Where warranted, an agency can also take disciplinary action against officials who have retaliated against a whistleblower. If the agency fails to do so, OSC can seek disciplinary action against the official by filing a complaint with the Board.

An Example of OSC's Work: The Port Mortuary Cases

An important matter early in my tenure as Special Counsel highlights how OSC can work with whistleblowers to shine a light a light on wrongdoing while protecting them from retaliation.

Three civilian Air Force employees at the Dover Port Mortuary disclosed to OSC that the mortuary mishandled the remains of fallen service members who died overseas. The whistleblowers also alleged that Air Force officials retaliated against them in response to their disclosures. OSC investigated and found that Air Force officials reprised against the whistleblowers, who faced removal, placement on extended administrative leave, suspensions, significant changes in duties and working conditions, and lowered performance appraisals after blowing the whistle.

When OSC presented its findings to the Air Force, the Air Force ultimately did the right thing. The whistleblowers were provided with full corrective action, and the officials responsible for retaliation were disciplined. The Air Force also reformed its mortuary operations and trained its employees on whistleblower protections. By working in collaboration with the Air Force, OSC was able to obtain relief for the whistleblowers and systemic changes without the need for litigation.

OSC's Ongoing Efforts to Help VA Whistleblowers

Cases from the VA comprise a large portion of OSC's workload, and I would like to briefly discuss our efforts regarding allegations of whistleblower retaliation at the VA.

OSC currently has about 125 active investigations of complaints from VA employees who allege retaliation for blowing the whistle on improper patient scheduling, understaffing of medical facilities, and other dangers to patient health and safety at VA centers around the country. To illustrate the growing number of VA cases, OSC has received over 80 new VA whistleblower retaliation cases related to patient health and safety just since June 1, 2014.

As our VA caseload rose rapidly this year, we reallocated OSC staff and resources and implemented a priority intake process. OSC representatives also personally met with numerous high-level VA officials, including the then-Acting Secretary, to emphasize the importance of these issues and discuss ways to work together on obtaining prompt relief for whistleblowers who suffered retaliation. OSC representatives also traveled to Phoenix to meet with a number of VA whistleblowers at the epicenter of the scandal. In addition, we have obtained several "stays," or delays, of disciplinary action against whistleblowers while we continue our investigations of these cases. Finally, OSC has coordinated with the VA to assist the agency in its efforts to educate and train its employees about whistleblower rights and protections.

The VA's leadership has been responsive and has worked with OSC to establish an expedited process to consider and settle meritorious whistleblower cases in order to provide these whistleblowers with relief as quickly as possible. In several cases, OSC has reached agreements in principle with the VA to provide whistleblowers with significant corrective action, and we are optimistic that we will be able to announce more good news soon.

OSC's Power to Delay Proposed Personnel Actions

OSC is able to protect complainants by seeking to stay proposed adverse personnel actions by filing formal requests with the MSPB. These stays provide temporary relief to federal employees while OSC investigates their claims. In addition, agencies can, and often do, agree to informal stay requests.

During the first two full years after my appointment as Special Counsel in 2011, OSC dramatically increased the use of informal stays. In 2012 and 2013, OSC obtained approximately 55 informal stays. In contrast, in the preceding five years (2007 to 2011), OSC obtained a total of 39 informal stays. When informal stays are not possible, OSC has also been more active in seeking formal stay requests with the MSPB.

For example, last month OSC obtained two formal stays from the MSPB in cases involving complainants at the Department of Agriculture and the Small Business Administration. In 2013, for the first time, OSC obtained stays on behalf of six former federal employees based on a novel theory of post-employment harassment. The employees claimed that they had been constructively discharged by their agency. None of the whistleblowers wanted to return to their old jobs. However, each wanted relief from the agency's continued efforts to force the employees to reimburse previously paid relocation bonuses. OSC requested an order from the MSPB to protect these former employees from this debt collection. Based on OSC's request, the Board granted the request for several of the employees and prevented the agency from seeking repayment of the bonuses.

Also, last year, OSC for the first time obtained a stay on behalf of an employee who faced retaliation for refusing to obey an order that would have violated the law. Specifically, the employee refused to follow an order to enter classified information into an unsecured computer network. The agency then placed the employee on a six-month detail out of the country, a decision that would cause the employee personal hardship and which the employee believed to be retaliatory. After OSC obtained an order from the MSPB to stay the detail, the agency agreed to discontinue the detail.

OSC's Alternative Dispute Resolution Program

As briefly mentioned earlier, OSC also refers selected prohibited personnel practice and USERRA complaints to mediation, a type of alternative dispute resolution (ADR). Under my tenure, OSC has greatly expanded our ADR program, which has been highly successful at resolving complaints to the mutual satisfaction of both agencies and complainants. For instance, in 2012, three employees of the Bureau of Alcohol, Tobacco, and Firearms who blew the whistle on Operation Fast and Furious resolved their cases through OSC's mediation program.

In fiscal year 2014, the settlement rate for mediated cases was approximately 75 percent. This is in addition to a high rate of corrective actions that are investigated and prosecuted at OSC, which result in corrective actions about 50 percent of the time. By comparison, complainants who go directly to the MSPB to litigate their claims receive corrective actions less than six percent of the time.

In addition to producing a high rate of corrective action, mediation also provides agencies and complainants with an opportunity to participate in the resolution of complaints. By taking on this productive role and working together to find solutions, the parties are more likely to have a higher compliance rate with the settlement—and, as importantly, work more productively together in the future. There is also a benefit to OSC when parties agree to mediate their cases. When cases settle through mediation, it obviates the need to investigate and prosecute meritorious claims, thereby saving OSC's limited resources.

III. Effect of the Whistleblower Protection Enhancement Act on OSC's Authority

The WPEA, which this committee worked hard to enact, has strengthened OSC's ability to protect whistleblowers. The WPEA's mandates include: a significant expansion of OSC's jurisdiction; a requirement to conduct investigations in hundreds of whistleblower cases that previously would have been dismissed; a direction from Congress to initiate more formal litigation and disciplinary actions against agency managers; and training requirements for all other government agencies. The WPEA also provides OSC with the authority to file *amicus* briefs in federal court cases that involve whistleblower protection issues.

One of the WPEA's changes is the creation of a thirteenth prohibited personnel practice, which prohibits agencies from imposing non-disclosure agreements that do not explicitly allow for whistleblowing. OSC has already successfully resolved at least two cases related to this new PPP, with relief that included supplemental training and removal of a reprimand.

The WPEA also clarified that a disclosure is not excluded from protection simply because it was made during the employee's normal course of job duties. As a result of this enhanced protection, OSC was able to obtain relief on behalf of an employee with the Department of the Army who was subjected to a retaliatory removal. The employee reported what she believed were violations of the Army's rules pertaining to the use of a government purchase card to her chain of command. Her report was made in the course of her duties. Shortly thereafter, the technician was fired. Prior to the WPEA, and as a result of Federal Court decisions, her report would have been excluded from protection as whistleblowing because it was made in the course of regular duties. The WPEA, however, overturned these decisions and OSC was able to pursue the case. As a result of OSC's investigation and report, the Army agreed to reinstate the employee with full back pay and benefits. It also convened a disciplinary review of the subjects responsible for the retaliatory discharge and is in the process of proposing disciplinary action.

The WPEA significantly improved OSC's ability to pursue disciplinary actions and we are taking action as a result. For example, in April, OSC filed complaints with the MSPB seeking disciplinary action against three Customs and Border Protection (CBP) officials. Our complaints accuse the three of discriminating for and against applicants based on political affiliation and granting illegal preferences or advantages to the preferred candidates. The complaints are currently pending before the Board. These disciplinary actions are OSC's first complaints against management officials for political discrimination in over 30 years.

As mentioned, the WPEA also expanded OSC's authority to file *amicus curiae* briefs in cases related to federal whistleblower retaliation. Prior to the WPEA, OSC had limited ability to file *amicus* briefs in whistleblower retaliation cases. Since receiving this expanded authority, OSC has filed three *amicus* briefs in federal appeals courts, including one this past month.

OSC first exercised its new *amicus* authority in *Kaplan v. Conyers*, arguing that the Federal Circuit Court of Appeals' decision threatened to undermine the enhanced whistleblower protections passed by Congress.

Then, in 2013, OSC filed an *amicus* brief with the Ninth Circuit in *Kerr v. Jewell*. OSC argued that the WPEA should be applied to cases pending before its enactment because: (1) it clarifies existing law by overturning prior decisions that unduly limited whistleblower protections; (2) Congress expressly intended the WPEA to apply to pending cases; and (3) applying the WPEA to pending cases promotes government efficiency and accountability. In its ruling, the Ninth Circuit determined that portions of the original Whistleblower Protection Act had been misapplied since its inception and that the WPEA simply clarified the protections Congress intended to confer in the statute.

This August, OSC filed an *amicus* brief with the Federal Circuit in *Clarke v. Dep't of Veterans Affairs*. OSC urged the court to reverse the MSPB's decision because it erected unnecessary procedural barriers for whistleblowers to meet in order to have their cases heard by the MSPB. This matter is pending.

Finally, OSC is currently considering filing an *amicus* brief with the U.S. Supreme Court later this month in *MacLean v. Dep't of Homeland Security*. This would follow the *amicus* brief we filed in Mr. MacLean's case with the MSPB in August 2011. Our concern in this case is that agencies might use regulations to create categories of disclosures exempt from whistleblower protections, contrary to the plain meaning and intent of the Civil Service Reform Act of 1978.

Our *amicus* briefs are meant to help courts interpret the contours of whistleblower laws, and we are optimistic that over time this will lead to a more pro-whistleblower body of jurisprudence.

IV. OSC's 2302(c) Certification Program

Government functions best and can address problems most effectively when employees feel comfortable and confident that they can blow the whistle at their agencies without retaliation. Creating this environment requires employees at all levels to be educated about their rights and responsibilities.

Federal agencies now have a statutory obligation to inform their workforces about the rights and remedies available to them under the WPA, the WPEA, and related civil service laws. OSC's 2302(c) Certification Program helps agencies meet this obligation through the following simple steps: agencies must place informational posters at agency facilities; provide information to new and existing employees and train supervisors about PPPs, the WPA, and the WPEA; and display a link to OSC's website on the agency's website or intranet.

To strengthen and expand whistleblower protections for federal government personnel, the Administration mandated participation in OSC's certification program under the White House's second National Action Plan on Open Government. Many agencies have contacted our office to begin the 2302(c) Certification Program process, and we keep an up-to-date list of all compliant agencies on our publicly accessible website. I am particularly encouraged that large agencies like the VA, the Energy Department, the Department of Health and Human Services, and NASA have taken steps to begin the certification progress.

Since my tenure as Special Counsel began, OSC has expanded its education and outreach efforts. In FY 2014, for example, we conducted 90 training sessions throughout the federal government. This compares with 33 sessions just three years ago. To help expand our education efforts in the federal workforce, we are also developing a new, online training quiz for federal employees that covers prohibited personnel practices, whistleblower disclosures, and the merit system principles. This quiz will allow us to educate a far larger portion of the federal workforce than in-person trainings alone. Better education can also help prevent retaliation from occurring in the first place.

Finally, OSC interacts with the federal community we serve through our website, which I am proud to announce we re-launched in July. We can now more easily communicate with federal employees. Filing complaints, making disclosures, and accessing information on our website is now easier. While we are pleased with the results so far, we are working to make further improvements. For example, we have been hard at work on a new online complaint filing system, which is designed to make it even easier for employees to report wrongdoing and ask for our help.

V.   Reauthorization

An issue for the subcommittee's consideration is the fact that OSC has not been formally reauthorized since 2007. Reauthorization provides Congress with an opportunity to evaluate OSC's authorities and responsibilities and make any necessary adjustments. At the Senate's request, we have provided recommendations for a range of legislative changes and would be pleased to provide this information to this Committee, as well.

Thank you for the opportunity to testify today. I look forward to answering your questions.

Mr. FARENTHOLD. Ms. Grundmann, the ball is in your court now.

STATEMENT OF SUSAN TSUI GRUNDMANN

Ms. GRUNDMANN. Thank you, Mr. Chairman, Ranking Member Lynch, distinguished members of this committee, including Congressman Cummings and Congresswoman Norton, who used to be my negotiations law professor back at Georgetown.

Good to see you again. I'm still sitting on the other side of the table.

Thank you for the opportunity to appear before you today and testify on behalf of the Merit Systems Protection Board. Let me acknowledge the presence of my distinguished colleagues and fellow Board members, the Vice Chair Anne Wagner, member Mark Robbins, and thank them for their strong contributions to fulfilling the Board's mission. It has been a great personal honor for me to serve with these two dedicated individuals.

Today we have been asked to discuss the Board's role in defending the merit principles and specifically our role in the appellate review of the Federal whistleblowers. We will address our recent observations of whistleblower appeals, the impact of the Whistleblower Protection Enhancement Act of 2012 on Federal employee whistleblowers and the Board itself.

The mission of the Merit Systems Protection Board is to safeguard, protect, and promote the merit principles through its statutory functions. One function is to adjudicate appeals filed by Federal employees. Under the Whistleblower Protection Act of 1989, the Board has jurisdiction over two types of appeals. One is referred to as IRA, an individual right of action. This appeal is of a nature that involves allegations of whistleblowing that are not directly appealable to the Board.

This means that before a whistleblower may file an IRA with the Board, that he or she is first required to seek corrective actions from the Office of Special Counsel. Generally, only after the Special Counsel investigates the claim and determines not to pursue corrective action is the employee then allowed to file an IRA with us.

The other time of whistleblower appeal is referred to as an otherwise appealable action. This type of appeal generally involves a claim that a personnel action, such as a termination or suspension, was taken in retaliation for whistleblowing.

In either type of appeal, the Board must determine whether the agency illegally retaliated against Federal employees for disclosing what the employee reasonably believes falls in one of four categories: One, a violation of law, rule, or regulation; two, gross mismanagement or waste of funds; three, an abuse of authority; four, a substantial and specific danger to public health or safety. Upon a ruling by the Board, an employee may then appeal to the U.S. Court of Appeals for the Federal circuit and, as a result of the Enhancement Act, at least till the end of this year, to any other court of appeals of competent jurisdiction.

We are currently aware of only four Board decisions on whistleblowing that have been appealed outside the Federal circuit. We understand that the House of Representatives has already passed legislation extending this provision an additional 3 years and that such legislation is now awaiting action in the Senate.

As to the number of whistleblowing appeals, any trends we may be aware of, since last fiscal year the number of whistleblower appeals has dramatically increased. What may be of interest to this subcommittee and particularly to Congressman Cummings is that the number of appeals jumped from 485 in fiscal year 2012 to 657 in 2013, after the enactment of the Enhancement Act. Whether there is a correlation between these two events we cannot say, but we can certainly say that Federal employees are filing whistleblower appeals with the Board more than at any other point in the last decade.

Regarding trends in whistleblowing appeals, we can say that as a result of the Enhancement Act, which greatly expanded the protections for whistleblowers by overruling a long line of cases by the Federal circuit, we understand that more whistleblower appeals are advancing to a hearing on the merits before administrative judges; that those hearings are much more detailed and lengthier in duration; and that more cases are obtaining a merits review by the full Board in Washington, D.C.

And while the numbers in our report in fiscal year 2013 are based on outcomes achieved under the prior law, and we look forward to fiscal 2014 which will provide a full year of data under the new Enhancement Act, already we can see the impact of the Enhancement Act in our cases. In our written statement we have included a list of precedential decisions issued by the Board under the new law. Of the 11 decisions listed, the appellant's case and claims succeeded in 6, all 6 of which were IRAs.

Another issue we believe of interest to the subcommittee is the Federal circuit's recent decision en banc in a case called Kaplan v. Conyers. The issue was simple: May the Board review an agency's determination that an employee is not eligible to occupy a position that is classified as noncritical sensitive. In that case, our agency argued that by limiting the Board's review in these types of appeals, that the Federal circuit's ultimate decision could have the effect of precluding whistleblower claims by employees in positions at issue. The Federal circuit dismissed this argument. The Supreme Court declined to hear the case. We understand that the House and Senate are considering legislation that would reverse this decision.

In addition to our adjudication function, the Board is tasked to conduct studies relating to the civil service and other merit systems in the executive branch. Since 2010 we've issued a series of reports, including one that may be of interest to Member Lynch, as we discuss a change in culture of agencies in order to allow whistleblowers to come forward.

In the near future, the Board is looking at studying the specific impact of the Whistleblower Protection Act of 2012, agency implementation of the act and the change of law in the landscape of the act.

This concludes my statement. I look forward to answering your questions. Thank you.

Mr. FARENTHOLD. Thank you very much.

[Prepared statement of Ms. Grundmann follows:]

Statement of

Susan Tsui Grundmann

Chairman, Merit Systems Protection Board

Before the

Subcommittee on the Federal Workforce, U.S. Postal Service, and the Census

of the

Committee on Oversight and Government Reform

House of Representatives

September 9, 2014

Good afternoon, Chairman Farenthold, Ranking Member Lynch, and other distinguished members of the Subcommittee on the Federal Workforce, the U.S. Postal Service, and the Census ("Subcommittee"). Thank you for the opportunity to appear before you today on behalf of the Merit Systems Protection Board ("MSPB" or "Board") and testify at this very important hearing. I would like to acknowledge my distinguished colleagues and fellow Board Members – Vice Chairman Anne Wagner and Member Mark Robbins – and thank them for their strong contributions to fulfilling the Board's mission. It has been a great personal honor for me to serve with these two dedicated individuals.

I have been asked to discuss the Board's role in defending the federal merit principles and specifically, the role the Board plays in the appellate review process as it relates to whistleblowers. In addition, I will provide information with respect to the number of whistleblower appeals filed at the Board over the past decade, discuss the impact of the Whistleblower Protection Enhancement Act of 2012, and address other issues that I believe will be of interest to the Subcommittee.

The MSPB And Its Role in Appeals Involving Whistleblowing

The MSPB is an independent, quasi-judicial agency within the executive branch of the federal government. The MSPB has four statutory functions:

1. To hear, adjudicate, or provide for the hearing or adjudication of all matters within the Board's jurisdiction, and to take final action on any such matter;
2. To order any federal agency or employee to comply with any order or decision issued by the Board, and to enforce compliance with any such order;
3. To conduct, from time to time, special studies relating to the civil service and to other merit systems in the executive branch, and report to the president and to the Congress as to whether the public interest in a civil service free of prohibited personnel practices is being adequately protected; and
4. To review rules and regulations of the Office of Personnel Management.

The Board is composed of three members, each appointed by the president, by and with the advice and consent of the Senate, not more than two of whom may be adherents to the same political party. It also employs numerous administrative judges at field offices around the county, who conduct first level review of appeals filed at the MSPB.

The mission of the MSPB is to protect the merit system principles and promote an effective federal workforce free of prohibited personnel practices. The most well-known statutory function of the Board is its role in adjudicating appeals of adverse personnel actions filed by federal employees.

Under the Whistleblower Protection Act, the Board exercises jurisdiction over two types of appeals filed by whistleblowers. The principal difference between the two is the manner in which they reach the Board for review:

Otherwise Appealable Action: In the first type of case, the individual is subject to an adverse personnel action that is directly appealable to the Board (e.g., removal), and the individual claims that the action was taken in retaliation for whistleblowing. This type of case is referred to by the Board as an "otherwise appealable action," and the individual may file an appeal directly with the Board after the action has been taken. In such an appeal, both the merits of the appealable matter (e.g., the removal action) and the claim of reprisal for whistleblowing will be reviewed by the Board.

Individual Right of Action: The second type of case was created by the Whistleblower Protection Act of 1989 and is referred to as an "Individual Right of Action." In this type of case, the individual is subject to a personnel action (e.g., denial of a promotion, or negative performance evaluation) and claims that the action was taken because of whistleblowing, but the action is not one that is directly appealable to the Board. The individual can appeal to the Board only if he files a complaint with the Special Counsel first and the Special Counsel does not seek corrective action on the individual's behalf.

In either type of whistleblower appeal, the Board must determine whether an agency illegally retaliated against a federal employee for making a "protected disclosure." A protected disclosure is one that the employee reasonably believed was:

- A violation of any law, rule, or regulation; or
- Gross mismanagement or a gross waste of funds; or
- An abuse or authority; or
- A substantial and specific danger to public health or safety.

Upon a final decision by the Board, an appellant is statutorily entitled to appeal to federal court for further review. In most instances, an appellant is required to appeal to the United States Court of Appeals for the Federal Circuit. Indeed, until the passage of the Whistleblower Protection Enhancement Act of 2012 ("WPEA"), the Federal Circuit retained exclusive jurisdiction over all whistleblower appeals from the Board. However, under section 108 of the WPEA, appeals from the Board may now be filed in either the Federal Circuit "or any court of appeals of competent jurisdiction." This "all circuit review" provision of the WPEA is set to expire in December 2014. The House of Representatives has passed legislation extending this provision for an additional three years, but the Senate has yet to act.

We are currently aware of only four whistleblowing decisions by the Board that have been appealed to courts other than the Federal Circuit under section 108:

- *King v. Department of the Army*, 2014 WL 2898536 (11th Cir. June 27, 2014) (No. 13-10301). The Eleventh Circuit affirmed the Board's decision denying Ms. King's request for corrective action under the Whistleblower Protection Act ("WPA") based on her allegation that she was not selected for positions with the Department of the Army because of a perception that she was a whistleblower.

• *Carson v. Merit Systems Protection Board*, No. 13-1273 (D.C. Cir. July 30, 2014). The D.C. Circuit affirmed the Board's decision dismissing for lack of jurisdiction Mr. Carson's whistleblower claim because he failed to make a non-frivolous allegation that the agency took a personnel action against him for making a protected disclosure.

• *Daniels v. Merit Systems Protection Board*, No. 13-73913 (9th Cir.). This case has been fully briefed and is pending before the Ninth Circuit. The issue is whether Mr. Daniel's disclosure that an administrative adjudicator's decision was legally erroneous was a protected disclosure of a violation of law, rule or regulation or a gross waste of funds within the meaning of the WPA.

• *Smith v. Merit Systems Protection Board & Department of Veterans Affairs*, No. 14-72578 (9th Cir.). This appeal was filed on August 18, 2014, and the case has not been briefed. The Board's decision dismissed for lack of jurisdiction Mr. Smith's whistleblower appeal because he failed to make a non-frivolous allegation that the agency took a personnel action against him for making a protected disclosure.

Whistleblower Appeal Data

From Fiscal Years ("FY") 2003 through 2006, the number of whistleblower appeals received by the Board decreased steadily, from 424 in FY 2003 to 319 in FY 2006. However, since FY 2007, the number of whistleblower appeals received by the Board has increased; from 391 in FY 2007 to 657 in FY 2013. The most notable increase occurred in the number of individual right of action appeals (IRAs) that were received in FY 2013. In that year, the Board received 418 IRA appeals, compared to 249 IRAs received in FY 2012. Whether this is a result of WPEA passage and enactment, we cannot say.

In accordance with Section 116(b) of the WPEA, the Board has begun to track the numbers and outcomes of whistleblower cases received and decided by the Board at the regional and headquarters levels. Inasmuch as the WPEA became effective in December 2012, this data represents only nine months of post-WPEA data for FY 2013. FY 2014 will be the first full year of data for appeals received and processed after enactment of the WPEA. Data for FY 2014 will be compiled and made available to Congress shortly after the end of the current fiscal year on September 30, 2014.

Of the 657 whistleblower initial appeals (both "IRA" and "OAA" appeals) the MSPB received in FY 2013, 103 were settled and 78 were adjudicated on the merits. In 32% of the appeals that were adjudicated (both "IRA" and "OAA" appeals), the appellants withdrew their allegations of whistleblowing. The Board did not rule in favor of the whistleblower in 63% of the appeals because: (1) the appellant had not made a protected disclosure under the law;(2) it determined that the protected disclosure was not a contributing factor in the personnel action; (3) it determined that the agency would have taken the same action in the absence of the protected disclosure; or (4) the appeal did not involve a "covered personnel action" under the law. Appellants were granted corrective action in 4 initial appeals (both "IRA" and "OAA" appeals) during FY 2013.

One noticeable trend that we have observed in these types of appeals is the increasing complexity of the allegations in the appeals. This increased complexity is the result of a combination of many factors, among them the WPEA, which broadly expanded the definition of a "protected disclosure," and the application of still good Federal Circuit precedent. The typical whistleblower appeal involves multiple allegations of several instances of alleged whistleblowing and several alleged retaliatory personnel actions. Thus, whistleblower appeals are often very difficult and time-consuming to analyze and decide.

Whistleblower Decisions by the Federal Circuit and the Board

We are aware of this Subcommittee's interest in the Federal Circuit's August 2013 *en banc* decision in *Kaplan v. Conyers*, 733 F.3d 1148 (Fed. Cir. 2013). The issue in *Conyers* was straightforward – does the MSPB have jurisdiction to review an agency's determination that an employee is not eligible to occupy a position that is classified as noncritical sensitive? *Id.* at 1150-51. The Federal Circuit ruled that the Board lacks jurisdiction to review the merits of such an agency determination, and instead may only review whether the employee received the procedural rights to which he or she was entitled under law. The MSPB, as a respondent in that case, argued that such a holding could preclude either review by the Board or a federal court of whistleblower claims by covered employees. The Federal Circuit dismissed this argument.

The full impact of the *Conyers* decision on whistleblowing in the federal government is not presently known. However, because the Supreme Court declined to review this case, any change to the law – as established by the Federal Circuit in *Conyers* – rests in the hands of Congress, not the MSPB. The Board is required to, and will, follow the decision of the Federal Circuit in this case.

Additionally, the Board has issued decisions in a number of appeals involving whistleblower allegations since the enactment of the WPEA. Among those decisions:

- *Day v. Department of Homeland Security*, 119 M.S.P.R. 589 (2013): The administrative judge ruled that the provisions of the WPEA providing protection to (1) disclosures made in the course of an employee's normal duties, and (2) disclosures made to the alleged wrongdoer did not apply to cases that were pending before the effective date of those provisions. The administrative judge reasoned that, under *Landgraf v. USI Film Products*, 511 U.S. 244 (1994), Congress had not clearly expressed an intention that the WPEA apply retroactively, and the WPEA standard for whether a disclosure is protected should not apply retroactively because doing so would have retroactive effect, i.e., would attach new legal consequences to events completed before its enactment. On interlocutory appeal, and after consideration of amicus briefs, the Board reversed, holding that the WPEA did not have an impermissible retroactive effect with respect to the above provisions of section 101 because it did not alter the parties' respective liabilities as Congress initially contemplated in enacting the WPA. The Board explained that the provisions of the WPEA at issue clarified, rather than effected substantive changes to, existing law, and thus did not raise concerns of retroactivity.

- ***King v. Department of the Air Force***, 119 M.S.P.R. 663 (2013): The administrative judge ruled that the provisions of the WPEA providing for compensatory damages (section 107(b)) did not apply to cases pending on the effective date of the WPEA. On interlocutory appeal, and after consideration of amicus briefs, the Board affirmed the ruling, applying *Landgraf* and finding that (1) Congress did not expressly define the temporal reach of section 107(b), and (2) retroactive application would be impermissible under *Landgraf* because it would alter the parties' respective liabilities as Congress initially contemplated them in enacting the WPA, and thus attaching new legal consequences for events completed before its enactment. The Board also held that section 107(b) cannot be applied retroactively because Congress did not expressly waive sovereign immunity for pre-enactment conduct, and that section 107(b) did not clarify the WPA.

- ***O'Donnell v. Department of Agriculture***, 120 M.S.P.R. 94 (2013): Applies section 101 of the WPEA in accordance with *Day* in finding that the appellant did not make a nonfrivolous allegation that his disclosure was protected. The Board held that the appellant's vague objections to an ineligibility ruling constituted a fairly debatable policy dispute that did not constitute gross mismanagement or a violation of law.

- ***Rumsey v. Department of Justice***, 120 M.S.P.R. 259 (2013): Applies section 101 of the WPEA to a pending case per *Day* in finding that the appellant's disclosures to her coworkers – that the state of Wisconsin submitted fraudulent data – were protected, even though they concerned matters within her job responsibilities. The Board ultimately ordered corrective action regarding the appellant's claims that the agency retaliated against her for her whistleblowing by cancelling her telework agreement and providing her with an improperly low performance rating.

- ***Schoenig v. Department of Justice***, 120 M.S.P.R. 318 (2013): Applies section 101 of the WPEA to a pending case per *Day* in finding that the appellant's disclosures – regarding potential fire code and workplace safety rule violations – were protected even though they appeared to be part of her normal duties and made through normal channels. After finding that the appellant also made a nonfrivolous allegation that her protected disclosures were a contributing factor in termination, the Board reversed the initial decision dismissing the appeal for lack of jurisdiction and remanded the appeal for adjudication on the merits.

- *Mudd v. Department of Veterans Affairs*, 120 M.S.P.R. 365 (2013): Finds that, although the WPEA extended the Board's IRA jurisdiction to claims arising under 5 U.S.C. § 2302(b)(9)(A)(i), i.e., the exercise of any appeal, complaint, or grievance right granted by any law, rule, or regulation with regard to remedying a violation of 5 U.S.C. § 2302(b)(8), the substance of the appellant's grievance did not concern remedying an alleged violation of subparagraph (b)(8). Thus, the Board lacked jurisdiction to consider an allegation that the agency took personnel actions in reprisal for the grievance.

- *Nasuti v. Department of State*, 120 M.S.P.R. 588 (2014): Applies section 101 of the WPEA to a pending case per *Day* and holds that under section 101 there is no requirement that the employee make a disclosure to a person who is in a position to remedy the matter disclosed. Finds jurisdiction over the IRA appeal and remands for adjudication on the merits upon finding that the appellant made a nonfrivolous allegation of a protected disclosure (substandard body armor being furnished to employees on route to Iraq) and that the disclosure was a contributing factor in his termination.

- *Clarke v. Department of Veterans Affairs*, 121 M.S.P.R. 154, ¶ 19 n.10 (2014): Notes that the WPEA amended 5 U.S.C. § 1221(e)(2) to provide that corrective action cannot be ordered if, "after a finding that protected disclosure was a contributing factor," the agency demonstrates by clear and convincing evidence that it would have taken the same personnel action in the absence of such disclosure. Holds that under this amendment the Board may not proceed to the clear and convincing evidence test unless it has first made a finding that the appellant established his prima facie case.

- *Hooker v. Department of Veterans Affairs*, 120 M.S.P.R. 629 (2014): Finds that section 101(b)(1)(A) of the WPEA, as it pertains to the prohibited personnel practice set forth at 5 U.S.C. § 2302(b)(9)(B) – the prohibition on taking a personnel action because of testifying for or otherwise lawfully assisting any individual in the exercise of a right referred to at 5 U.S.C. § 2302(b)(9)(A) – would not be applied to a case that was pending when the WPEA was enacted because under *Landgraf* doing so would increase a party's liability for past conduct as compared to pre-WPEA liability. Although no new duties were imposed, because such conduct was previously prohibited under the WPA, the WPEA did increase a party's liability for past conduct by creating a new Board appeal right in IRA appeals alleging such conduct.

- *Carney v. Department of Veterans Affairs*, 2014 WL 3845217 (Aug. 6, 2014): Finds that the appellant engaged in protected activity under the WPEA, 5 U.S.C. § 2302(b)(9)(b), based on a claim of retaliation for representing a coworker in a grievance proceeding. Because all of the actions relevant to consideration of whether the agency retaliated against the appellant in violation of 5 U.S.C. § 2302(b)(9)(B) occurred after the December 27, 2012 effective date of the WPEA, the Board did not have to address the retroactivity of that provision in light of *Hooker*. Finds jurisdiction over the appeal and remands for a hearing on the merits.

- ***Benton-Flores v. Department of Defense***, 121 M.S.P.R. 428 (2014): Finds that when an appellant has made a protected disclosure in the normal course of her duties, the WPEA at 5 U.S.C. § 2302(f)(2) now requires her to prove that the personnel action taken was in retaliation for the disclosure, i.e., that the agency took the personnel action with an improper retaliatory motive. Thus, there is an additional evidentiary burden for appellants who have raised such claims. Remands for further adjudication on this issue after finding jurisdiction over the IRA appeal and finding that the appellant is entitled to a hearing on the merits.

Board Reports on Whistleblowing

In addition to the MSPB's adjudication function, which is discussed above, MSPB is statutorily required to conduct studies relating to the civil service and other merit systems in the executive branch. We are pleased to report that since 2010, MSPB has issued a series of reports on the topic of whistleblowing:

- **Whistleblower Protections for Federal Employees**. September 2010. This report addresses the legal challenges that whistleblowers face, including case law of the MSPB and the Federal Circuit, and describes the requirements for a Federal employee's disclosure of wrongdoing to be legally protected as whistleblowing under current statutes and case law.

- **Prohibited Personnel Practices: Employee Perceptions**. August 2011. This report describes what each "prohibited personnel practice," including illegal retaliation for whistleblowing, means as a practical matter, how frequently federal employees perceive each practice occurring, and the consequences for an agency when its employees believe that management is committing one or more prohibited personnel practices.

- **Blowing the Whistle: Barriers to Federal Employees Making Disclosures**. November.2011. This report compares data from Merit Principles Surveys conducted in 1992 and 2010 to describe the extent to which perceptions of retaliation against federal employees who report wrongdoing remains a serious problem. The report also explains why agencies should do more to ensure that employees receive quality training about how they can disclose wrongdoing and how they can exercise their rights if they perceive that they have experienced retaliation for whistleblowing activities.

Finally, the MSPB will be holding an open "Sunshine Act" meeting next week to discuss MSPB's proposed research agenda and to determine which issues it will report on over the next four years. One topic that the Board is currently considering for a future report, and which will be discussed at the Sunshine Act meeting, is the state of whistleblowing after the enactment of the WPEA in 2012. If selected, this study would build on previous MSPB research and examine changes in whistleblower case law since 2010, with a focus on how the WPEA has changed the landscape.

This concludes my written statement. I thank the Subcommittee for the opportunity to testify and look forward to answering your questions.

Mr. FARENTHOLD. Mr. MacLean, look forward to hearing your story.

STATEMENT OF ROBERT MACLEAN

Mr. MACLEAN. Thank you, Mr. Chairman and Ranking Member Lynch and Ranking Member Cummings.

I was in the first class of 35 air marshals to graduate after the 9/11 attacks of 2001. In 2003, a perfect storm hit. All marshals were called in for emergency training. Al Qaeda hijackers would exploit U.S. Department of State visa and checkpoint screening loopholes in order to sneak weapons onto long haul flights, kill crews, and crash their jets. Briefers were specific to major U.S. east coast cities and European capitals.

Two days later, TSA blasted out an unmarked text message to all marshals' unsecured cell phones: Cancel all hotel reservations to avoid all cancellation fees. Flights for 4 hours or longer wouldn't have marshals for 2 months until TSA got its new fiscal year funds. Marshals around the country told me that they got the same text. We thought it was a mistake, given the alert and a very specific law that 9/11-type flights must be covered.

I called the supervisor, who confirmed TSA formed a global plan because it was broke. I called three IG offices until I spoke to an agent detailed from FEMA. He just warned me about risking my career. Since the text was not specific, it was not marked nor secured, I called a reporter covering TSA's dangerous rules. He verified with marshals across the country and was in contact with Congress. The story went on the Web.

Hours later most press had coverage of outraged bipartisan Members of Congress, including Hal Rogers, the Republican chairman with the oversight of the TSA. After first denying it, TSA said it made a mistake and canceled its plan before ever taking effect. The IG said that TSA blew cash on executive bonuses.

Weeks later I cofounded the air marshal chapter of the Federal Law Enforcement Officers Association, FLEOA. It's not a union, but a collective voice to work with Congress and agency officials to better safety and security. The Air Marshal Service Director asked the IG to investigate me and my FLEOA air marshal board for complaining about hazardous policies. He called us organizational terrorists.

For 2 years we worked with Chairman Jim Sensenbrenner's Judiciary Committee. In 2006, he issued a 147-page report about the Air Marshal's dangerous policies and retaliation against us FLEOA representatives. None of this was considered retaliatory, because the director and his executive who fired me, Frank Donzanti, later testified that they were all at one time FLEOA members.

Mr. Donzanti told me I was under suspicion for disclosing unclassified sensitive security information or SSI. Internal Affairs ordered me to divulge all media I was a source for. I admitted to everything, as it was all unclassified at the time and everyone agreed with me, Congress, bipartisan. But a decade later, I've been second-guessed in hundreds of briefs and hearings and depositions.

Dumbfounded for 19 weeks, TSA finally concocted its single charge to fire me. The text message it chose not to send to our $22 million encrypted smart phone system was now SSI. TSA forced its

SSI chief in charge when I made my disclosure not to show up for his ordered deposition and replaced him with an attorney who was with the Postal Service when I made my disclosure. TSA was a little nervous. Its attorneys interrupted him 252 times during his deposition. This was the TSA's expert on SSI, who didn't come to the TSA long after I made my disclosure.

Mr. Donzanti was the only witness allowed at my hearing 3 years later. Everyone else was denied. Despite unbelievable excuse why he didn't have the authority to ground me for almost 5 months, the fact that he was permanently removed from all supervisory duties just weeks after my hearing, Mr. Donzanti's credibility was never scrutinized.

Despite a precedential decision, a unanimous Ninth Circuit Court of Appeals panel ordered that TSA's 2003 program's lack of clarity must be considered, but all of the TSA's SSI experts were blocked from my hearing. Last year, in another precedential decision, the Court of Appeals for the Federal circuit unanimously ruled I did not violate any laws and ordered a new hearing to determine if I had a reasonable belief of any wrongdoing. The government en banc appealed that decision to every Federal circuit judge. It was denied unanimously.

Finally, Mr. Chairman and Ranking Member Lynch, TSA took my testimony out of context to cancel the Ninth Circuit's unprecedented—I'm sorry—it was unanimous, good faith belief order, it quoted me as saying that it didn't matter to me if I disclosed SSI to the public. But what the transcript reveals is that I stated that it did not matter if I disclosed SSI to my supervisor. It was a perfect cut-and-paste job. With that, the government now argues in its current appeal to the Supreme Court of the United States that I, quote, ''intentionally released sensitive security information,'' unquote. My oral arguments before the Supreme Court are on November 4.

I look forward to answering your questions. Sorry for going over time.

Mr. FARENTHOLD. You didn't do too badly.

[Prepared statement of Mr. MacLean follows:]

TESTIMONY OF ROBERT MACLEAN

before the

HOUSE OVERSIGHT AND GOVERNMENT REFORM COMMITTEE,

SUBCOMMITTEE ON FEDERAL WORKFORCE, U.S. POSTAL SERVICE AND THE
CENSUS

September 9, 2014

Mr. Chairman:

Thank you for inviting my testimony. My name is Robert MacLean. Currently my Whistleblower Protection Act case is the first involving the Act that will be heard by the Supreme Court. But I am not here to talk about the legal arguments. I want to share why I had to blow the whistle, and what it means for our country to protect the freedom to warn. The timeline below shares a whistleblowing experience I never wanted to have. But it forced me to make the most difficult choices and decisions of my life, about my duty to the country as a public servant and law enforcement officer. The timeline below chronicles a series of events that has changed my life forever, and may have been even more significant for our nation's safety.

1992 — After four years as a nuclear weapons specialist, I was honorably discharged from the Air Force with a Top Secret clearance and the option to reenlist.

1996 — I became a Border Patrol Agent in the San Diego Sector. Not to be confused with a port inspector you see working at land border entry points or airports. I patrolled the vast area between entry points.

32 days after the 9/11 attacks — I was specially recruited to be in the first class of U.S. Federal Air Marshals (Air Marshals) to graduate after the 9/11 attacks.

July 26, 2003 — Four months after the invasion of Iraq, all Air Marshals throughout the country were recalled for mandatory unprecedented in-office emergency suicidal Al-Qaeda hijacking training. We were briefed that terrorists planned to exploit a visa and foreign security screening loophole in which weapons would be smuggled onto aircraft to neutralize the crew and fly jets into east coast cities, Europe, and Australian targets. The scope was far broader, and the consequences could have been far more severe, than 9/11.

But two days after our emergency training and just days before the anticipated hijackings, the Transportation Security Administration (TSA) sent an unsecured, unmarked, unclassified text message to ALL Air Marshals to cancel all hotel room reservations in order to avoid late-cancellation fees. All long distance missions requiring overnight stays by air marshals would be cancelled. TSA chose to send the unlabeled text message to our unsecured Nokia 3310 cellular phones instead of our $22 million encrypted smart phone system. There were no markings or secrecy restrictions on the message.

I confirmed with other Air Marshals around the U.S. that they received the same text message. We all thought it was a joke given the special training we had just received and the post 9/11 law that nonstop long-distance flights were a priority. I first went to a supervisor who confirmed to me that the agency was financially broke and the national plan was directed by headquarters. But he said there was nothing I could do, and to just leave it alone.

In the Air Force and Border Patrol every telephone had fluorescent stickers with a 1-800 Inspector General hotline to report "fraud, waste, and abuse." I called the Department of Homeland Security OIG hotline to report I was concerned about the TSA's plan to cancel air marshal coverage during a hijacking threat. I eventually reached a criminal investigator, who also told me there was nothing he or I could do. He also warned me about the possibility of cutting my career short if I pursued the issue further.

I couldn't give up. To get the word to Congress, I reached Brock Meeks of MSNBC, who verified the text message with other Air Marshals around the U.S., contacted Congress, and issued a story about the TSA order on MSNBC's homepage the night of July 29 -- just days before the anticipated hijacking.

The next day President Bush could not defend the action at a morning briefing, and there were press conferences with Senators Hillary Clinton, Chuck Schumer, and Barbara Boxer on CNN, Fox News Channel, and MSNBC. They were mercilessly ripping the TSA's plan.

Senator Boxer said during the new conference: "I want to thank the air marshals who came forward and told the truth about what was going on within their agency and bringing this issue into the spotlight... "

Senator Chuck Schumer of New York said: "Given the potential fallout of another attack that intelligence reports suggest is on the way, it is incredible that the TSA would consider reducing the air marshal presence on these flights simply to save the cost of an overnight hotel room."

After denying the plan for several hours following the MSNBC story, TSA told USA Today that it made "a mistake". Less than 24 hours after the story broke, TSA proceeded to cancel its plan before it ever took effect.

The U.S. Government Accountability Office and the Department of Homeland Security Inspector General later issued reports about TSA's plan. They discovered that I made my disclosure five days before the terrorist attacks were scheduled. The plan had intended to leave nonstop, long distance flights unprotected for two months— August 3, 2003 until September 30, 2003.

A few weeks after, I co-founded the air marshal chapter of the Federal Law Enforcement Officers Association (FLEOA). It was time to unify our voices. TSA would retaliate against my fellow FLEOA air marshal board members, such as Spencer Pickard. Mr. Pickard would eventually be forced to resign after appearing on ABC News 20/20 about a two-year House Committee on the Judiciary investigation we initiated and cooperated with. It titled the report:

"In Plane Sight: Lack of Anonymity at the TSA Federal Air Marshal Service Compromises Aviation and National Security". The report confirmed FLEOA whistleblowing disclosures of mismanagement that caused gross security breaches, exposing the identity of undercover agents. For example, the agency let a hotel chain advertise its undercover Air Marshals as its "guests of the month."

On September 9, 2004 I appeared behind a screen on an NBC Nightly News television program about a series on what was not being done to protect the public since the September 11, 2001 attacks. TSA managers conducted an investigation to identify who had blown the whistle. On May 4, 2005, in an interview with DHS criminal investigators, I admitted to being a source of the 2004 NBC Nightly News TV show, as well as the 2003 disclosure to MSNBC. I specifically denied releasing any classified or "Sensitive Security Information."

For almost five months, the TSA took no action against me. It did not place me on restrictive duties, suspend my TOP SECRET security clearance, place me on administrative leave, nor did it revoke my access to an Internet portal with numerous Air Marshal schedules and seating assignments for nine months. But then it officially labeled the unmarked text message as Sensitive Security Information after the fact, and on April 11, 2006, it fired me for breaching national security due to "Unauthorized Disclosure of Sensitive Security Information." I've now spent over eight years in legal battles, seeking to end the punishment for correcting the agency's "mistake" the only way that was left: warning Congress and the public.

I've paid a high price for doing my duty. Not so much in terms of legal fees, because so many have come to my support, from FLEOA to the Government Accountability Project to former Acting Solicitor General Neal Katyal. But in terms of everything else, it has been a disaster to "commit the truth."

So why did I do it? I blew the whistle, because I had to. I could not live with the tragedy risked if I had been the cynical silent observer. When we think about why our movement matters, put yourself in my place and ask yourself, "What if I had remained silent?" I believe that I made a difference by blowing the whistle to defend our country. It would be an honor to work with your committee to make a difference so that whistleblowers can defend themselves.

Mr. FARENTHOLD. Dr. Van Boven, you're recognized here for 5 minutes.

STATEMENT OF ROBERT VAN BOVEN

Dr. VAN BOVEN. Thank you. I'm a physician scientist——

Mr. FARENTHOLD. Could you make sure your microphone is turned on there. There's a button there. It says "talk" on it.

Dr. VAN BOVEN. I'm a physician scientist and was a director of the Department of Veterans Affairs Central Texas Traumatic Brain Injury Research Program in Austin from 2007 to 2009. Beginning in 2002, the VA and the University of Texas agreed to jointly build a brain imaging center in Austin and the VA invested $6.3 million. The center was opened in January of 2006, but recruiting for a director did not start for 6 months. I was recruited a year and a half later, in July. Troop deployments at the time were averaging 22,000 servicepersons per year with 6,000 TBI victims annually.

With over 300,000 military TBI casualties worldwide since 2000 and 2 million annual civilian cases, advances to make these invisible wounds visible and to develop effective treatments for TBI were and remain to be sorely needed. With training at Harvard, Northwestern University, and 7 years postdoctoral research at Hopkins and the NIH, I felt this was a perfect opportunity for a neurologist scientist to make a difference.

But within weeks at the helm, I learned that 2.1 million, approximately one-third of the funds provided to the BIRL, or Brain Imaging and Recovery Lab, had already been spent on ghost staff, as well as unqualified administrative clinicians performing noncredible diabetic research unrelated to TBI. He depended on the technical support of a semiretired research contractor who hadn't published in 10 years. He had been fired from his immediate past employer and engaged in billing which I believed to be fraudulent. The team had not collected any data for 10 months, findings that were subsequently confirmed by the OIG.

Now, my efforts to terminate the contracting services and invalid research were overruled. My protest resulted in calls for my resignation and involuntary reassignment under a person I accused of wrongdoing. The retaliation and counterclaims that followed were akin to Kafka's "The Trial." False allegations were withheld from me. I was not able to confront witnesses. Evidence of retaliatory animus by those accused of wrongdoing were stricken from the scope of investigations, and I was found guilty without an opportunity for defense.

An Administrative Board of Investigation was manipulated with brazen disregard for VA policies and due process and fairness, and an ABI called in response to my complaints was later amended to add a long list of counterclaims. Patriotism was also punished; that is, I was condemned for volunteering to organize a 5K run for wounded warriors with Governor Perry, Willie Nelson, and 1,000 Americans.

Later, the ABI scope and justice itself was turned upside down. The scope is now restricted to allegations against me. The new ABI was reconvened despite an ongoing OIG investigation, which is violation to VA policies, its chair was a past subordinate of an official alleged with wrongdoing, and during the ABI hearing any mention of senior management misconduct or waste was stymied. The chief of staff was also authorized by the VA headquarters to be the deciding authority for a grievance against him, and this chief of staff found himself not guilty.

After removal from the BIRL in 2008, I was banned from oversight of my own human studies, posing risk to the subjects and violating all kinds of VA policies. The center was idle but still burning money. It was moved to Waco in July of 2009, and most of the 6.3 million was spent without studying or helping a single veteran. Many of my complaints to the OIG and the ORO were substantiated by these investigations, in part prompted by Washington Post coverage.

The ABI grievance hearings and a VA Summary Review Board defied the Whistleblower Protection Act's principles and engaged in unjust practices in their own right, and did a good job of it. The VA attempted to suppress information from Congress. Moments before the Merit Systems Protection Board hearing, VA officials asked if I would stop initiating contact with Congress and others for a settlement.

Settlement was accepted because I was advised that corrective action by the Merit Systems Protection Board was unrealistic. In fiscal year 2013, the MSPB granted 4 out of 657 persons, that is less than 1 percent, with corrective action after adjudication for appeals with whistleblower reprisal claims. Even after my termination the VA continued to engage in harmful retribution, blacklisting me with marathon persistence.

Past failings in transparency and mismanagement are indeed prologue. VA officials later testified before Congress again in 2010 falsely claiming that personnel in Waco, with a director who had a nicotine expert, had TBI and neuroimaging expertise, hence justifying the BIRL's closure. I had been contacted by a Waco whistleblower later that told the opposite story, and he was persecuted for it, and indeed, I referred him to the Government Accountability Project and he's being represented them.

Four years later, deceit was revealed. A second failed program now, overseen by the same officials that oversaw the BIRL, is covered in the obituary section—I mean the front pages, it may as well have been the obituary section—of the Austin Statesman this past Sunday. The article points out that the two imaging programs, the BIRL and Waco, cost taxpayers $12 million and squandered a decade of opportunity.

Ironically, through a congressionally directed medical research program award, one of three in the Nation, I and colleagues at MIT, UCSF, and the Department of Defense are now helping and carrying out a treatment trial at Fort Hood. That's covered by the Sentinel.

So with over a billion dollars a year in research budgetary resources and appropriations and the same for medical support like the BIRL, scrutiny of the VA research management program in oversight appears worthy.

Now, in conclusion, delivering help to those who are afflicted with brain disorders from TBI and post-traumatic stress disorder is dependent on good science and integrity. I'm a clinician. I take care of people with brain injuries daily. However, if a culture fights rather than fosters transparency, that suppresses rather than rises to the opportunity for improvement, then the infamous stereotypes will continue to curse the VA bureaucracy and degrade the whistleblower alike, and the public will suffer. Whistleblowers have their roots in stopping crime. They need your protection from persecution and denigration so they can help transparency, integrity, and performance in government today.

I thank you.

Mr. FARENTHOLD. Thank you very much, Doctor.

[Prepared statement of Dr. Van Boven follows:]

STATEMENT

OF

ROBERT W. VAN BOVEN, M.D., D.D.S.

BEFORE THE

HOUSE OF REPRESENTATIVES

COMMITTEE ON OVERSIGHT AND GOVERNMENT REFORM

ON

EXAMING THE ADMINISTRATION'S TREATMENT OF WHISTLEBLOWER

SEPTEMBER 9, 2014

Chairman Issa, Congressman Cummings, and distinguished members of the Subcommittee, it is my honor to appear before you today to testify about my whistleblowing experiences about my experiences making unwelcomed disclosures of gross waste and mismanagement and retaliation that followed as a physician –scientist and former director of a Department of Veterans Affairs (VA) traumatic brain injury imaging (TBI) research center in the at Austin Texas from 2007-09. I pray that this testimony and accompanying exhibits may contribute towards a better appreciation of the need for more protection of those who witness wrongdoing or gross mismanagement in government so that they do not fear retribution for speaking out. *Suppressing this freedom will undercut transparency, integrity, and the ability of government to fulfill its mission- to serve the people.*

Beginning in February 2002, the VA and University of Texas at Austin (UT/A) agreed to jointly create a "world-class university-based brain imaging center" housed at UT's Research Campus in Austin. The VA put $6.3 million toward its startup. An opening ceremony for the imaging center was held in January 2006; but the VA did not begin recruiting for a Director until 6 months *after* the center opened.

I was recruited in July 2007, 1 ½ years after the center's opening and appointed "Physician-Medical Director of the VA Austin Imaging Center." At the time, U.S. Troop deployments were averaging 22,000 servicepersons per year during the periods of 2006 through 2009 with an alarming average of 6,000 TBI victims diagnosed annually. To date, the Defense and Veterans Brain Injury Center (DVBIC) estimates over 300, 000 military TBI casualties worldwide since 2000. Moreover, civilian TBIs were being increasingly appreciated, with more than 2 million cases occurring annually. The Brain Imaging and Recovery Laboratory (BIRL) was borne out of this pressing need to better detect, that is to make this "invisible" wound *visible*, and effective treatments for TBI.

With neurology training at Harvard and Northwestern University, and seven years combined postdoctoral research at the Johns Hopkins Hospital and advanced brain imaging work at the National Institutes of Health (NIH), this was a perfect opportunity to make a difference in the lives of those who suffer from cognitive and emotional problems from brain injuries.

But within weeks of my start in July 2007, I learned that $2.1 million, more than 1/3rd of the funds provided to the BIRL, had been spent, including unchecked support of an unqualified investigator performing non-credible research (subsequently panned by 5 external experts),for research that was also unrelated to TBI and specific needs of veterans. This funding was also provided, not on scientific merit or productivity, but for an unrelated administrative quid-pro-quo that superiors expressly feared would otherwise lead to their dismissal. A contractor's billing practices were also highly suspect, substandard, and plagiarized, causing to his release from his recent past employer. These problems were continuing to siphon critical resources, already dwindled by the waste of the preceding years. Left un-remedied, this trajectory would ruin the renewed mission of the center- to help those with traumatic brain injury.

My disclosures to VA administrators, beginning on September 20, 2007, fell on deaf ears and resulted in intimidation (e.g. calls for my resignation), suppression (e.g. requests for me to retract and electronically erase my disclosures from Research Committee review), and retaliation (e.g. loss of fiduciary and staffing authority as Director, and later involuntary reassignment under a person I filed disclosures against, and threats of increased clinic duties).

Retaliation methods and counterclaims

My attorney, Tom Devine of the Government Accountability Project (GAP), likened my case to Kafka's *The Trial*, prosecution by an inaccessible authority, with the nature of my crimes withheld from me. An Administrative Board of Investigation (ABI) was requested on February 4th by the COS to the Central Texas Veterans Health Care System (CTVHCS) Director based on my February 1st disclosures of waste, mismanagement and administrative misconduct. Counter-claims were added by administrators and I was removed from the BIRL and detailed to sole clinical responsibilities on February 6, 2008.

After my removal from the BIRL, I was banned from oversight of my own human research protocols, in violation of VA research policies and also posed risks to human research subjects. This prompted my VA Office of Research Oversight (ORO) complaint in March 2008 and immediate suspension of all research.

The lab was again dormant scientifically for another 1 ½ years, just as it had existed 1 ½ years prior to my arrival, burning fuel (i.e. taxpayer dollars) like an idling jet. No clinical research was ever conducted and the BIRL was "moved' to Waco in July 2009 with most of the $6.3 million burned-up without studying or helping a *single veteran*.

I then filed complaints with the VA's (Office of Inspector General) OIG on February 5, 2008, the Office of Special Counsel (OSC) in February 2008, Congress, the media (initially February 2008), and the VA's Office of Research Oversight (ORO) in March 2008. Many significant allegations were affirmed by these investigations.

Despite my complaint to the VA's OIG, the ABI plans proceeded in violation of VA policies which require abeyance of OIG investigations (e.g. criminal investigation for fraud). I protested to Mr. Shea, VISN 17 Director, to no avail. More counter-claims were added to an ABI charge letter sent by the on February 15th. After reporting this violation of non-abeyance to the OIG, these investigators notified the ABI convening authority (VISN 17) on February 26, 2008 to suspend the ABI pending the completion of the OIG investigation.

The ABI and VA's Summary Review Board (SRP) suppression and/or disregard for due process and compelling evidence of prohibited personnel practices exacted by VA officials were staggering. These retaliatory practices continued after my removal from the BIRL and detail to exclusive clinical duties from February 2008 until my suspension in September 2009. These investigative and review bodies, in close collusion with overseeing officials from VA headquarters, *engaged in unjust practices in their own right*, revealing clear retaliatory animus for my disclosing concerns of VA improprieties.

During this ABI suspension, the VISN 17 Director serving as ABI convening authority then communicated a lack of counterclaim evidence to justify an ABI against me to the Chief of Staff (COS), a target of both the OIG and ABI investigations. *The COS then engaged in witness tampering,* in violation of the February 26th OIG abeyance order to solicit more allegations and evidence (see witness letter of Dr. Greg Harrington).

The ABI was later re-activated by a new convening authority, Ms. Joleen Clark, Chief Workforce Management and Consulting and Joseph Pomorski, VA HR Consultant, *before the OIG completed its investigation. Ms. Clark then turned the ABI charge and scope upside down.* All of my allegations (e.g. senior manager misconduct and dereliction of duties, waste and mismanagement), prompting the ABI in February, 2008 were tossed out and relegated to an inappropriate *grievance hearing* decided upon by a person (Mr. David Wood) at a subordinate level to a person accused of misconduct (VISN 17 Director for complicity in witness tampering).

When I attempted to appeal to this aberration of justice, Mr. Pomorski declared no appeal of ABI change was possible and suggested I "drop the grievance." When I complained to Mr. William Feeley office, the former Deputy Under Secretary for Health , Operations and Management was, according to the COS "furious." The COS delivery of Mr. Feeley's refusal to intervene was personally delivered while I was treating patients, He was accompanied by a VA police escort, in the presence of patients and staff. When I filed a grievance protesting Dr. Sherwood's humiliating action, he was hardly unbiased in the matter. He was authorized by Pomorski and Clark to serve as deciding authority in the grievance I filed against him (see exhibit-May 30, 2008 VA Memorandum) and rejected the grievance out of hand, after having "thoroughly and carefully considered" of my grievances against him.

The ABI was a biased tribunal. When I attempted to provide evidence and a basis for retaliatory animus by CTVHCS leadership, the ABI Chair (Dr. William H Campbell, Deputy Chief of Staff, South Texas Veterans Health Care System) chastised me and complained about me in his report, stating "*He repeatedly went off on tangents to provide commentary on matters that were beyond the scope of the ABI, such as the alleged abuse of funds by the CTVHCS leadership.*" Some allegations were *withheld altogether* from me at the ABI, I was judged "guilty" of these withheld allegations by the ABI and I only learned of these at the time of "sentencing" by the Summary Review Board (SRB), i.e. the termination proceedings. Counterclaims against me included:

• Insubordination for defying orders to refrain from organizing a fun run to benefit traumatic brain injury research – even though a letter from the VA regional counsel opined that I was free to organize the event as a private citizen.

• Hanging a personalized door tag outside of my office –even though permission was granted to purchase it at my own expense.

• The use of profanity and engaging in "threatening gestures" at work. I admitted that I occasionally used profanity at work or socially but never used a "threatening gesture" or ever directed profanity toward a person.

• "Disrespecting" Sen. John Cornyn at a BIRL event attended by the senator. The VA alleges I disrespected the senator by allowing the event to run long in order to allow two wounded veterans not on the agenda to speak. Cornyn's office wrote a letter denying that Cornyn felt disrespected. Indeed he stayed and took photos with the veterans.

• Sexual harassment. A subordinate claimed that he overheard asked a female UT researcher about unprotected sex. The researcher, who does not work for Van Boven, wrote a letter *vehemently* refuting the accusation. This sensational lie was a distortion from when my team was reading and reviewing surveys to select for behavioral screenings.

Bartering for silence

Twice the VA attempted to barter for silence of the whistle. At the October 15, 2008 Summary Review Board (SRB) sentencing hearing, Dr. Arana, one of three members asked if I would cease whistleblowing activity if I were to remain at the VA. The SRP declared I was "unsalvageable" as I did not promise to keep silent if wrongdoing persisted. Minutes before starting the MSPB lawsuit trial in District Court in Dallas, the Administrative Judge demanded the unwilling VA to discuss settlement. The VA then asked if they paid a settlement, whether I would stop initiating contact with Congress, the media, and veterans groups. Settlement terms were then negotiated and reached in December, 2010. When I expressed trepidation to the terms of the VA offer for settlement, my attorney explained that "take it because the remedy rate with the MSPB is unjust.

The terrible performance of the MSPB in 2010 has not seen any substantial change since the passage of the WPEA in 2012. In FY 2013, a representative year, the MSPB only granted 4 persons with corrective action after adjudication out of 657 individuals who submitted initial appeals with whistleblower reprisal claims. *These statistics cannot credibly be suggested to reflect the true incidence of those subjected to prohibited personnel practices.* http://www.mspb.gov/netsearch/viewdocs.aspx?docnumber=996058&version=999982&application=ACROBAT *The right to a jury trial would enhance transparency and justice and should replace the MSPB.*

Post-termination retribution

Retributions did not end with my termination in January 2009, or even after the VA settlement *nearly two years later.* Despite the arduous but the successful Merit System Protections Board (MSPB) IRA appeal, filed in December 2009 by my counsel, Mr. Tom Devine of GAP, and VA Settlement in November 2010, retaliations persisted for years.

1. On February 18, 2009 the VA unduly reported me to the National Practitioner Data Base (NPDB), indicating that I was "terminated" for "unprofessional conduct." One month later, *upon media inquiry* on March 5, 2009 to the VA, Diane Struski, the VISN 17 Executive Assistant and Public affairs officer declared that my termination was *not* reportable to the clinician database and the NPDB report was strangely *expunged the very same day.*

2. The only peer-reviewed publication generated from the BIRL was a 34 page comprehensive review on advanced imaging of TBI and post-traumatic stress disorder (PTSD) which I labored on under the duress of a 60 day stay-of -termination and submitted on December 8, 2008. But even this scientific contribution was nearly thwarted. The invited editor for special TBI/PTSD issue of the VA's *Journal of Rehabilitation Research and Development* (JRRD) called and alerted me that he had been *discouraged against accepting the paper* by Stacieann Yuhasz, Editor for the Journal. Her reasoning was not based on scientific merit, but on a VA headquarters official's concern over a June 2009 *Washington Post* article exposing the closure of the BIRL.

3. When I secured employment and was appointed Director of the TBI Clinic at Fort Riley Kansas, media attention to VA waste and whistleblower retaliation claims triggered retribution and abrupt discharge as a contractor at the hands of Great Plains Regional Medical Command of the Army. VA officials later reached out to DOD Command at Carl R. Darnall Army Medical Center at Fort Hood and made disparaging remarks on August 3, 2010, expressing displeasure over my presence in the DOD (see letter to President Obama and OSC_Post_VA retaliation)

What's past is prologue.

After the July 2009 closure of the BIRL, VA officials testified before Congress in 2010, falsely arguing that redundancy in MRI and TBI expertise (the opposite was at the heart of the Waco failure) at Waco justified the BIRL closure and emphatically "ensure[d] a robust Veteran-focused neuroimaging.....[research program in] traumatic brain injury in Central Texas" [see DVA Memorandum 7 February 2013]. These VA officials that testified before Congress oversaw more than 3 ½ years of waste and closure of the BIRL in the wake of my disclosures, and remained in power to oversee 6 more years of failure at the "Center of Excellence" brain imaging program in Waco. http://projects.statesman.com/news/va-center-of-excellence/austin.php

As reported in this past weekend's issue of the Austin American Statesman, the July 1, 2008 Waco unveiling of a MRI scanner "once hailed by VA leaders as the most powerful mobile MRI on the planet" has not led to a single study published since its acquisition 6 years ago. http://projects.statesman.com/news/va-center-of-excellence/ The article argued that the unused "Center of Excellence" and MRI at Waco "devolved into a ghost machine [and] stands as a stark symbol of the VA's shortcomings in responding to the specialized needs of soldiers returning from the longest-running conflicts in the country's history."

The article further points out that between the BIRL and Waco (both part of CTVHCS and VISN17), "the two imaging programs cost taxpayers more than $12 million and squandered almost a decade of opportunity." With more than $1 billion-a-year in research budgetary resources (including $ 586 million from direct appropriations and the same from medical care support- source of BIRL funds) scrutiny of VA research management and oversight appears worthy of review.

Conclusions

Dr. Michael Merzenich, one of our nation's leading neuroscientists, Professor Emeritus at UCSF, Member of the National Academy of Sciences and the Institute of Medicine observed the following about the VA's response to quality issues I raised about the organization.

> I have read the Inspector General offices report, and found it to express a lot of what is wrong with the VA and our bureaucracy. It chooses to hide behind legalisms to deny the obvious. The obvious is that before Dr. Van Boven joined this group, this unit was administered by incompetent non-research professionals supervised by equally incompetent administrators who chose to frustrate rather than support his attempts to turn a

dysfunctional research unit into a vibrant, world-class contributor to research that had high promise for helping soldiers and returning veterans in great NEED of that help.

Ironically, from the ashes of two failed VA TBI neuroimaging programs over eight years, a Central Texas TBI neuroimaging and treatment trial has emerged from the thanks to a Congressionally Directed Medical Research Program DOD TBI treatment trial award, one of three in the nation, being conducted at Fort Hood. This effort is one I attempted to launch 8 years ago at the BIRL and is being conducted in collaboration with colleagues at MIT, UCSF, Brook Army Medical Center and Fort Hood,
(see http://www.forthoodsentinel.com/story.php?id=14179; also see http://clinicaltrials.gov/ct2/show/NCT01908647)

Delivering help to those who are afflicted with brain disorders from TBI and PTSD is dependent on good science and integrity. However, if a culture fights, rather than fosters transparency; that suppresses, rather than rises to opportunities for improvement; then the infamous stereotype will continue to curse the VA bureaucracy and whistleblower alike, and the patient and public will suffer.

Respectfully submitted,

Robert W. Van Boven, M.D., D.D.S.

Mr. FARENTHOLD. And I did see the article in the Statesman this weekend after the Texas football game. It was much more interesting than the sports pages.

Mr. DEVINE. Could you get your microphone, too, please, sir?

STATEMENT OF TOM DEVINE

Mr. DEVINE. Thank you, sir. I'm the legal director of the Government Accountability Project. We're a nonpartisan, nonprofit whistleblower support organization that since 1977 has helped over 6,000 whistleblowers and been a leader in the campaigns to pass or defend nearly all Federal whistleblower laws.

We're also a founding member of the Make It Safe Coalition, which is the tip of an iceberg for a unique, trans-ideological, bipartisan solidarity consensus between voters and whistleblowers. Our coalition recruited over 400 organizations and corporations with some 80 million members to support passage of the Whistleblower Protection Enhancement Act. They ranged some from the Center for American Progress, Common Cause, the unions, Public Citizen, to the Liberty Coalition, the National Taxpayers Union, the Taxpayers Protection Alliance, the Competitive Enterprise Institute, the American Conservative Defense Alliance, and the American Policy Center. This is an unprecedented mandate for the values of your hearing.

But for whistleblowers, the nearly 2 years since passage of the WPEA have been the best and the worst of times. There's unfinished business and how it is resolved will complete the struggle. I'd like to summarize five areas where there are challenges or hard work left to achieve the act's promise.

The first is the sensitive jobs loophole. The decision that Chairman Grundmann summarized by the Federal Circuit Court of Appeals, Kaplan v. Conyers, has created the most significant threat to the merit system that has kept the civil service professional and nonpartisan since 1883.

I won't repeat the arguments that the chairman made, but where the dust has settled is that the government now has uncontrolled power to designate virtually any job in the government as sensitive. The Federal circuit applied the principle to those who stock sunglasses at commissaries, and proposed regulations by the Office of Personnel Management would permit designation for all jobs that require access to either classified or unclassified information. In other words, all jobs that require literacy are sensitive now.

Sensitive employees will no longer be entitled to defend themselves through an independent due process hearing, and there are no consistent procedures for justice within the agency. The bottom line is this is a structure to replace the merit system with a functional blank check for a national security spoils system. That is simply unacceptable.

Second is the MacLean case that Mr. MacLean has testified on. He testified on what happened to him. I'd like to testify on the significance to the WPEA.

This November, the Supreme Court will hear its first WPEA case, Whistleblower Protection Act case, since the law was enacted. At stake are the two most basic significant premises for this law. First, that only Congress can restrict public whistleblowing disclosures, not the agencies who allegedly engaged in fraud, waste, abuse, illegality, or activities threatening the public. Otherwise, wrongdoers would have the right to gag whistleblowers exposing their own misconduct. Second, when Congress restricts public whistleblowing disclosures, it must do so with specificity. Otherwise, employees will have to guess whether they have legal rights when they serve the public's right to know and uncertainty creates an inherent chilling effect.

An adverse ruling would cancel everything that we had accomplished in the Whistleblower Protection Enhancement Act. We believe a congressional friend-of-the-court brief from Mr. Cummings, as well as others at the Federal circuit, made a major difference in the results, and we're recruiting participants for a congressional friend-of-the-court brief to the Supreme Court.

The third issue is circumventing the whistleblower protection rights by making it a crime to blow the whistle instead of an employment offense. The war on whistleblowers goes well beyond unprecedented Espionage Act prosecutions. Since passage of the WPEA, we've seen a stark shift from traditional employment actions to criminal investigations and prosecutive referrals. Increasingly, whistleblowers are given the choice of resigning or risking jail time.

Ernie Fitzgerald once nicknamed whistleblowing as committing the truth because you're treated like you committed a crime, and this literally is becoming the new reality. It's not surprising. Criminal investigations are much easier and less burdensome than multiyear litigation. There's no risk of losing. All you have to do is close the case. And the chilling effect of facing jail time is much more severe than facing an adverse action. This problem could easily be fixed by codifying legislative history through the 1994 amendments of the WPEA.

And finally, there are pending WPEA issues that are confronting us. They're confronting us from the remainder of the Whistleblower Protection Enhancement Act, whether there should continue to be normal access to appeals court, whether civil service employees like corporate whistleblowers should have access to court in a jury trial if they don't get timely rulings, and whether the MSPB should have summary judgment authority.

There is also hard work to continue and resume from OSC–MSPB reauthorization. In 2007, this committee prepared legislation and marked it up through subcommittee to make over and modernize these institutions, which haven't had that upgrade since 1978. Further action was postponed until the WPEA, and it is time to roll up our sleeves and get to work on it.

Mr. Chair, the WPEA was landmark legislation to restore rights that Congress has now passed unanimously four times since 1978. But the pressure to enforce abuses of secrecy through silence also is timeless, trans-ideological and bipartisan.

The WPEA's most significant issues have not yet been resolved, and agency creativity is already producing new, more intimidating forms of harassment. The rules that govern the merit system procedures are increasingly becoming out of date. Our work isn't finished, and the whistleblower community and GAP stands ready to do our share.

Mr. FARENTHOLD. Thank you very much, Mr. Devine.
[Prepared statement of Mr. Devine follows:]

TESTIMONY OF THOMAS DEVINE,
GOVERNMENT ACCOUNTABILITY PROJECT

before the

HOUSE OVERSIGHT AND GOVERNMENT REFORM COMMITTEE,

SUBCOMMITTEE ON FEDERAL WORKFORCE, U.S. POSTAL SERVICE AND THE
CENSUS

on

WHISTLEBLOWER PROTECTION SINCE PASSAGE OF THE WHISTLEBLOWER
PROTECTION ENHANCEMENT ACT

September 9, 2014

Mr. Chairman:

Thank you for inviting my testimony. My name is Tom Devine, and I serve as legal director of the Government Accountability Project ("GAP"), a nonprofit, nonpartisan, public interest organization that assists whistleblowers, those employees who exercise free speech rights to challenge abuses of power that betray the public trust. GAP has led or been on the front lines of campaigns to enact or defend nearly all modern whistleblower laws passed by Congress, including the Whistleblower Protection Act of 1989 (WPA) and 1994 WPA amendments, as well as the Whistleblower Protection Enhancement Act of 2012 (WPEA).

Our work for corporate whistleblower protection rights includes those in the Sarbanes-Oxley law for some 40 million workers in publicly-traded corporations, the 9/11 Commission Act for ground transportation employees, the National Defense Authorization Act for all government contractors, including defense contractors, that are outside of the intelligence community, the Consumer Product Safety Improvement Act for some 20 million workers connected with retail sales, the Energy Policy Act for the nuclear power and weapons industries and AIR 21 for airlines employees, the Dodd-Frank Wall Street Reform and Consumer Protection Act for financial-sector employees, the Affordable Care Act for health care workers and patients, among others.

We teamed up with professors from American University Law School to author a model whistleblower law approved by the Organization of American States (OAS) to implement at its Inter American Convention against Corruption. In 2004 we led the successful campaign for the United Nations to issue a whistleblower policy that protects public freedom of expression for the first time at Intergovernmental Organizations, and in 2007 analogous campaigns at the World Bank and African Development Bank. GAP has published numerous books, such as The Whistleblower's Survival Guide: Courage Without Martyrdom, The Corporate Whistleblower's Survival Guide: A Handbook for Committing the Truth, which won the "International Business Book of the Year" award at the 2011 Frankfurt Book Fair, and law review articles analyzing and monitoring the track records of whistleblower rights legislation. See: Devine, *The Whistleblower Protection Act of 1989: Foundation for the Modern Law of Employment Dissent*, 51 Administrative Law Review, 531 (1999); Vaughn, Devine and Henderson, *The Whistleblower Statute Prepared for the Organization of American States and the Global Legal Revolution Protecting Whistleblowers*, 35 Geo. Wash. Intl. L. Rev. 857 (2003); *The Art of Anonymous Activism* (with Public Employees for Environmental Responsibility and the Project on government Oversight)(2002); and Devine, *Running the Gauntlet: The Campaign for Credible Corporate Whistleblower Rights*, (2008).

Over the last 37 years we have formally or informally helped over 6,000 whistleblowers to "commit the truth" and survive professionally while making a difference. This testimony shares and is illustrated by painful lessons we have learned from their experiences. We could not avoid gaining practical insight into which whistleblower systems are genuine reforms that work in practice, and which are illusory.

Along with the Project On Government Oversight, GAP also is a founding member of the Make it Safe Coalition, a non-partisan, trans-ideological network of 50 organizations whose members pursue a wide variety of missions that span defense, homeland security, medical care, natural disasters, scientific freedom, consumer hazards, and corruption in government contracting and procurement. We are united in the cause of protecting those in government who honor their duties to serve and warn the public. Our coalition led the citizen campaign for passage of the Whistleblower Protection Enhancement Act.

Our coalition was just the tip of the iceberg for public support of whistleblowers. Community organizations and corporations have signed a letter to President Obama and Congress to give those who defend the public the right to defend themselves through the same model as HR 1507 -- no loopholes, best practices free speech rights enforced through full access to court for all employees paid by the taxpayers. It is enclosed as Exhibit 1. The breadth of the support for HR 1507's approach is breathtaking – including good government organizations ranging from Center for American Progress, National Taxpayers Union and Common Cause, environmental groups from Council for a Livable World, Friends of the Earth and the Union of Concerned Scientists, conservative coalitions and organizations such as the Liberty Coalition, Competitive Enterprise Institute, American Conservative Defense Alliance and the American Policy Center, to unions and other national member based groups from American Federation of Government Employees and the National Treasury Employees Union, to the National Organization for Women.

This hearing is particularly significant, because for whistleblowers the nearly two years since passage of the WPEA have been both the best and worst of times. There is unfinished business from the WPEA, and how it is completed will resolve the struggle. My testimony below summarizes five areas where there are new challenges or hard work left to achieve the Act's promise.

I.   THE SENSITIVE JOBS LOOPHOLE.

A decision by the Federal Circuit Court of Appeals (Federal Circuit), which the Supreme Court has declined to review, has created the most significant threat to the civil service merit system in our lifetime. In *Kaplan v. Conyers,* 733 F.3d 1148 (Fed. Cir. 2013), *cert. denied* 2014 U.S. LEXIS 2280 (U.S. Mar. 1, 2014). The courts have declined to interfere with policies by the last two presidents to create a "sensitive jobs" loophole that could eliminate independent due process rights for virtually the entire federal workforce. The roots of this doctrine are a McCarthy era regulation creating a prerequisite security check for those who hold jobs that do not currently but some day may need a security clearance for access to classified information. Although the practice had been long dormant, it has been revived by the last two presidents for implementation throughout the Executive branch.

In the aftermath, the government has uncontrolled power to designate any position as "sensitive." The Federal Circuit applied the principle to those who stock sunglasses at commissaries, and proposed regulations by the Office of Personnel Management (OPM) and Office of the Director of National Intelligence (ODNI) will permit the designation for all jobs that require access either to classified or unclassified information. "Sensitive" employees will no longer be entitled to defend themselves through an independent due process proceeding at the Merit Systems Protection Board (MSPB); and there are no consistent procedures to achieve justice within agencies. Already workers are being removed for old debts or other financial problems, despite having good credit without significant current debt – even if financial hardship were a valid basis to purge the civil service. In effect, we are on the verge of replacing the merit system with a national security spoils system. This would provide absolute authority over nearly two million workers to the most secretive, wasteful bureaucracy in government, whose surveillance abuses already have created a national crisis for freedom.

For the moment, the Administration has not challenged WPEA or employment discrimination rights for sensitive job holders. But those rights are crippled, if employees cannot defend their innocence against underlying charges. And based on past experience with the security clearance loophole to civil service law, prohibited personnel practices will be the inevitable next domino to fall. It is only a matter of time.

Congress has begun to counterattack. Both the House, through Representative Eleanor Holmes Norton, Ranking Member Elijah Cummings, Representative Robert Wittman and other bi-partisan sponsors; and the Senate through companion legislation have proposed legislative action to fill this newest, potentially all-encompassing loophole to the merit system. Quick action is essential, or there will be a cumbersome, expensive, time-consuming challenge to reconstruct the civil service. Already some agencies have begun converting their entire workforce to sensitive jobs. GAP's associated friend of the court brief to the Federal Circuit, and public comments on the OPM/ODNI proposed new rules are attached as Exhibits 2 and 3.

II.   UPCOMING *DEPARTMENT OF HOMELAND SECURITY v. MACLEAN* SUPREME COURT DECISION.

When Congress enacted the Whistleblower Protection Enhancement Act, original sponsor and House floor manager Todd Platts expressed his concern over a potential new loophole that could be created from the case of Robert MacLean, a Federal Air Marshal (FAM) who exercised the freedom to warn, and prevented the government from canceling all FAM coverage during a confirmed, more ambitious rerun of the 9/11 terrorist hijacking attack.

An adverse decision would cancel the two most basic, significant premises for WPA free speech rights: 1) Only Congress can restrict public whistleblowing disclosures, not the agencies who allegedly engaged in illegality, fraud, waste, abuse, mismanagement or activities creating a threat to public health or safety. Otherwise, wrongdoers would have the right to gag whistleblowers exposing agency misconduct. 2) When Congress restricts public whistleblowing disclosures, it must do so with specificity. Otherwise, employees will have to guess whether they have legal rights when they serve the public's right to know. Uncertainty creates an inherent chilling effect that would defeat WPEA's purpose of encouraging public disclosures when government officials breach the public trust.

As Mr. Platts stated,

[A]gencies must not be allowed to circumvent whistleblower protections through so-called "secrecy" regulations, such as a new category of information (labeled "Sensitive Security Information") created by the Department of Homeland Security. Whistleblower law understandably already exempts from whistleblower protections information which is classified or "specifically prohibited by law" from release. Classified information is information that is kept secret by Executive Order, not a hybrid category of information created by agency regulation like ''Sensitive Security Information.'' Moreover, ''prohibited by law'' has long been understood to mean statutory law and court interpretations of those statutes, not to agency rules and regulations.

If the Federal Circuit Court broadens the ''prohibited by law'' exemption to include anything that an agency tries to keep secret under any of their regulations, a new loophole could be opened up that would substantially under- mine Congressional intent in passing this bill. It is therefore important to once again make it clear: ''Prohibited by law'' has long been understood to mean statutory law and court interpretations of those statutes, not to agency rules and regulations. Any exception to these rights must be created by Congress, and Congress must act with specificity. That has been the law since 1978, and it continues to be the law.

Cong. Rec. (Sept, 28, 2012), at E1664

Unfortunately, while the Federal Circuit agreed with Mr. Platts unanimously in two rulings, the Department of Homeland Security and the Department of Justice did not, and they persuaded the Supreme Court to hear their appeal. An adverse ruling would cancel all the open government gains in the WPEA. A congressional friend of the court brief to the Federal Circuit is attached as Exhibit 4.

III.   CIRCUMVENTING THE WPEA BY MAKING IT A CRIME TO BLOW THE WHISTLE.

The Obama Administration has been harshly, justifiably criticized for a "War on Whistleblowers" through unprecedented Espionage Act prosecutions for allegedly leaking or preparing to leak classified information. In reality, the phenomenon is much broader. As a service organization, GAP cannot avoid becoming sensitive to the latest patterns of retaliation. Since passage of the WPEA, we have seen a sharp shift from traditional employment actions to criminal investigations and prosecutive referrals. Increasingly, whistleblowers are given the choice of resigning, or risking jail time. Ernie Fitzgerald once nicknamed whistleblowing as "committing the truth," because you're treated like you committed a crime. Increasingly, instead of isolating or firing whistleblowers, that literally is becoming the new reality for whistleblowers.

That is not surprising. First, criminal investigations are much easier and less burdensome than multi-year litigation with teams of lawyers, depositions, hearings and appeals. All it takes is an investigator who is proficient at bullying. Second, there is no risk of losing. In a worst case scenario, an agency merely closes the investigation (and can open up a new probe on a new pretext at any time). Third, the chilling effect of facing jail is much more severe than facing an adverse action.

Criminal witch hunts are the most effective means available to scare employees into silence, but under current law it is uncertain whether WPA anti-retaliation rights are applicable.

In legislative history, 1994 WPA amendments designated retaliatory investigations and prosecutive referrals as threatened personnel actions creating WPA rights, but so far no ruling has applied that legislative history.

To avoid WPEA rights being neutralized through a pretextual criminal backdoor, Congress must codify its longstanding intent to nip this ugliest form of retaliation in the bud, before it can lead to criminal proceedings. A GAP briefing packet on the issue is enclosed as Exhibit 5. Our white paper on the phenomenon, *Whistleblower Witch Hunts*, is enclosed as Exhibit 6.

IV.   UNRESOLVED WPEA ISSUES.

Three contentious WPEA issues were postponed for resolution until after a four year study by the Government Accountability Office (GAO) – 1) whether a two year experiment in normal "all circuits review" should be extended permanently as a substitute for the Federal Circuit's' prior monopoly; 2) whether civil service employees should have access to court, as an alternative to administrative hearings when there is not a timely ruling; and 3) whether the MSPB should have summary judgment authority to rule against whistleblowers without an administrative due process hearing. Nearly two years have passed, and it is overdue for the GAO to begin serious research.

All circuits review: The House already has begun to do its share by unanimously approving the All Circuits Review Extension Act, which expands the pilot program to five years so that GAO will have time to complete its study. The Senate Homeland Security and Governmental Affairs Committee unanimously approved companion legislation. Notwithstanding responsible rulings in the MacLean case, the Federal Circuit still has not ruled in favor of a whistleblower for a final decision on the merits since passage of the WPEA nearly two years ago. Normal appellate due process is a necessity, or Congress may well have to pass the same whistleblower rights a fifth time.

District court access: Since 2002 Congress has passed twelve whistleblower statutes, all providing for *de novo* jury trials in district court if the employee does not receive a timely administrative ruling. This was necessary, because the administrative hearing system does not have the structure, resources or time for cases with the most public policy significance, and/or involving complex or highly technical issues. That applies equally or more to resolution of civil service whistleblower cases, but the widespread mandate for district court access was blocked by threat of a Senate procedural hold. The GAO study should provide the empirical basis for this long overdue, responsible and proven reform.

Summary judgment authority: The MSPB long has sought this authority to more efficiently manage its docket. Whistleblower groups led by civil rights organizations, however, have strenuously resisted, because it has been badly abused at the Equal Employment Opportunity Commission in discrimination cases. The threat of a guaranteed hearing always has been the whistleblower's only significant leverage to settle cases. There never has been a significant chance for success on the merits or settlement after hearing, due to a long, deeply ingrained track record of hostility by Administrative Judges.

V.   OSC-MSPB REAUTHORIZATION.

While the WPEA clarified and restored rights against retaliation, this legislation is necessary to make the remedial agencies more accessible and user friendly in practice. Quite simply, in a structural and procedural level, too often they have become dysfunctional since their creation in 1978. In 2007, this committee prepared HR 3551 to begin the makeover, and the bill was marked up in subcommittee. Further action was postponed, however, until passage of the WPEA. It is time to resume serious work on modernizing these agencies to address lessons learned.

For whistleblowers, the most significant provisions in HR 3551 were –

* reforms to permit joinder of related cases with common facts instead of requiring separate proceedings;

* realistic standards to obtain temporary relief, the key to timely and fair settlements, by providing it whenever a whistleblower proves a *prima facie* case of retaliation; and

* an independent process for accountability when Special Counsels abuse their power.

Discussions by the Office of Special Counsel (OSC) and good government organizations with senate staff have produced a consensus for further reforms in a renewed effort through –

* mandatory regulations by the OSC, which has not issued them since its 1978 creation;

* a two year statute of limitations for employees to file prohibited personnel practice complaints;

* OSC authority to issue and enforce subpoenas;

* increased employee access to evidence in case files, in exchange for fewer OSC burdens to explain decisions;

* enfranchisement of whistleblowers in framing the issues when OSC orders an agency investigation into their disclosures;

* OSC authority to monitor agency corrective action commitments in response to whistleblowing disclosures; and

* an expanded OSC certification program for agency training in merit system principles.

This work is significant and must be completed to modernize increasingly antiquated agency structures and practices. GAP is committed to any contributions necessary for its share.

Mr. Chairman, the WPEA was landmark legislation to restore rights that Congress now has passed four times since 1978. But the pressure to enforce abuses of secrecy through silence is timeless, trans-ideological and bi-partisan. The WPEA's most significant issues have not yet been resolved, while agency creativity already is producing new, more intimidating forms of harassment. At the same time, the rules that govern practices at merit system remedial agencies increasingly are becoming out of date. We hope that the committee will take advantage of willingness by GAP and other good government organizations in the 50 member Make It Safe Coalition to reach the WPEA's mandate by finishing the toughest reform issues, and modernizing the Act's implementation.

Mr. FARENTHOLD. I'll now recognize myself for the first round of questioning.

Ms. Grundmann, I believe it was Dr. Van Boven pointed out what struck me as an incredibly low success rate that whistleblowers have in front of your agency. Are those numbers accurate? And what are some of the reasons that whistleblowers typically lose when they're before you guys?

Ms. GRUNDMANN. Let me address the first issue. The numbers are what they are, but as I said in my opening statement, those numbers are reflective of the cases that were adjudicated under the old law. So we're closing out on our fiscal year numbers for 2014 that will fully reflect how the law has impacted the outcome.

I believe your second question is——

Mr. FARENTHOLD. So you're saying that those numbers reflect past law?

Ms. GRUNDMANN. Right. Right.

Mr. FARENTHOLD. So let's step into current. I realize you all haven't completed the numbers.

Ms. GRUNDMANN. Right.

Mr. FARENTHOLD. I'd like to see those numbers when they're done. But at least anecdotally, can you give me some idea why the whistleblowers are losing all the time.

Ms. GRUNDMANN. Under the old law, it's quite apparent, which is why Congress changed the law. In addition, in changing the law, the Whistleblower Protection Enhancement Act, this Congress overruled a long series of cases by the Federal circuit which we were obligated to follow since they are our reviewing court.

For reasons why they prevail, we really don't track why particular individuals prevail. We do track when cases are dismissed. A number of cases are filed untimely. A number of cases are dismissed because of failure to exhaust the administrative remedies through the Office of Special Counsel. There could be a number of other reasons which we don't track. We are a very small organization.

Mr. FARENTHOLD. So now, Mr. Devine, you're head of an advocacy organization. Does somebody track the reasons people lose there? Does somebody read the cases? Microphone, please, sir. Could you turn your microphone on, please, sir.

Mr. DEVINE. Yes, we do track the cases, and the WPEA is requiring the Merit Board to give much more detailed statistics and analysis of the causes.

I'd like to say that while we haven't agreed with all the Board's rulings, this Board is unsurpassed at the leadership level, at the top, for fairness, objectivity, and honest interpretation of the law. The problem that we've seen is more at the administrative judge level.

The Board is not designed with the resources or the time to hear complex cases. The judges have to finish these cases in 120 days, and it's not always realistic when we're talking about major breakdowns in the system. And they don't have the political independence to challenge misconduct at higher pay grade levels than the judges frequently are. It's not designed for the cases that are the most significant for the WPEA.

54

It would be very helpful if the administrative judges were required in the OSC–MSPB reauthorization to get some intensive training on the importance of this act and its mandate and what it means, and if they were upgraded from being just administrative judges to administrative law judges with more independence from political pressure.

Mr. FARENTHOLD. All right. And, Dr. Van Boven, I've never ceased to be stunned at what comes out of the VA. I mean, we've just had a huge scandal with wait lists and long wait times. It's something that we struggle with in my office in a lot of the casework that we do for individuals.

I understand you're now separated, but I assume you still have some friends and contacts there. I know it's been barely a month since the President assigned the reforms that we passed out of this House and the Senate passed. Is it getting better? Are we just spinning our wheels up here? Microphone, please.

Dr. VAN BOVEN. I think that with firm determination and leadership, top-down culture leadership and accountability, that it will set an example and I think that it can occur. The problem is, Mr. Devine just alluded to, it's that there are stodgy indoctrinated pieces of the fabric that need to be, to mix metaphors, diarrhoeased. We need an enema.

The thing is that you're wondering about why that 1 percent prevails, and I applaud the Merit Systems Protection Board's statement of saying the numbers are what they are. God bless her. Because the point is, once we open our eyes, and it's all about transparency, and none of us like to admit our own transgressions, that I'm saying hate the sin but not the sinner. So I think, look, we can always change.

That gets to the next point: Why do those people prevail? I'll tell you why they prevail. Because it was just like that line from ''Mr. Smith Goes to Washington,'' he says basically—I'm paraphrasing, I was trying to look it up—he says, I'm never going to quit. He says, someone will listen to me eventually.

Well, I felt the same way. When the VA tried to settle with me or make me go away, they said, Dr. Van Boven, it's been 4 years with you, it's been like round 13. I said, are you kidding me? I was bluffing. I said this is round one. I was broke and unemployed. I said, I'm going to make this my life passion. So I think real solid determination.

You know, Sam Houston said, do right and risk the consequences. This man did right and he risked the consequences. And whether or not what a court says or what the hearings come out to say and how many people vote for it or against it, it doesn't matter, because 120 years ago we said it's okay to have slaves. They were wrong. And I think the same thing goes here. Once we open our eyes and say we've got to do something, then change will happen.

Mr. FARENTHOLD. Thank you very much.

I see my time has expired, actually, over by a minute and a half, so I'll recognize Mr. Lynch for 6–1/2 minutes.

Mr. LYNCH. Thank you, Mr. Chairman.

Ms. Lerner, you got some data, though, in your testimony you shared with us regarding the old system and the new system under the WPEA. I know you didn't drill down on some of your written testimony, but what do you see in terms of, as Ms. Grundmann has indicated, there has been a spike in appeals, but you've also got some results, I think, right?

Ms. LERNER. That's right. I mean, I—my microphone is on, right? I think you can look at it in a couple of different ways. To give it some perspective, I think that the rising numbers can be viewed as a very good thing. For one thing, people aren't going to come forward unless they feel like they're going to be protected from retaliation.

And our numbers of complaints have gone through the roof. We, as I mentioned, have about 5,000 this year, and those are increases in both disclosures of waste, fraud and abuse, and health and safety issues, and retaliation complaints. So more people are coming forward to make disclosures. More people are coming forward with complaints. But I think those are actually good things. Whistleblowers who are coming forward are having more of an impact than at any time in our agency's history.

And a couple other points. The numbers are also increasing, I think, because of changes at OSC. We've been very aggressive in trying to protect whistleblowers. The staff is using every tool that we have available to us to curb waste, fraud, and abuse, and we've had some very high-profile cases.

And when we talk about changing the culture, when you get strong results, either through systemic changes like we've been able to see at the VA and the Department of Homeland Security and the Air Force and the FAA, that's a message that gets out to all Federal employees, that they can make a difference.

The other message that gets out is when you discipline people they see the consequences of retaliating, and the Whistleblower Protection Enhancement Act has given us the tools that we need to bring disciplinary actions, and I think that that will also have an effect.

Education and outreach is also very important, and the fact that the administration is now requiring all agencies to go through our certification process I think is also going to have a very positive affect on culture.

Mr. LYNCH. All right. If the person who complains is not there the next day, then that's a pretty strong signal that the administration is sending out there that that's not a good career move to speak up and to complain about the way things are being done.

I do want to just take a step back and just say, I thought the testimony here, across the board, every single one of you has, I think, offered very thoughtful and important testimony, very helpful to me, I think.

Mr. Devine, you laid out those five points or five issues that you wanted to raise, the first one being—what was it—sensitive job loophole. Do you think it is worthwhile for Congress to try to define that legislatively or would judge-made law, would that suffice?

Mr. DEVINE. Unfortunately, Mr. Lynch, that's the only solution that's left. We've run out of options in the courts. And the civil service merit system will have to be legislatively reborn independent of the national security sensitive job——

Mr. LYNCH. Not the answer I wanted to hear. I was trying to come up with a definition of sensitivity that would really provide the fullest recourse for whistleblowers. And I think about Dr. Van Boven at the VA dealing with patients and patient records and confidential information. And it's right across government. I mean, the more important work we're doing would obviously ring that bell for sensitivity and close down the recourse of complaining employees. We're going to have a real struggle with that and we've got to figure a way to do that.

Mr. DEVINE. It's going to be tough, but I don't know, sir, if it's necessary to come up with a new definition of sensitivity with respect to civil service rights. That concept comes from the McCarthy era in 1954 and it's been dormant. It's been in a coma until the last two administrations, which have revived it. And the normal boundary for sensitive jobs has been when you have access to classified information. Classified information is very broadly defined. And that's work, and there haven't been any even accusations that it hasn't worked. This is simply a power grab to shift control of employment rights from the civil service system to officials with national security blank checks.

And your point about the VA is very well taken. Unfortunately, we've been representing VA whistleblowers since the 1990s and things are not getting better there. We're very grateful that the Office of Special Counsel, has made this the first time in its history, has selected a whole agency to investigate for prohibited personnel practice, because they permeate it.

The gentleman who came after Dr. Van Boven, Dr. David Tharp, who carried on his dissent for the next $12 million that didn't produce any research, the veterans groups have twice made him, in the last 4 years, twice made him the DAV employee of the year, he is so outstanding. The harassment of him was so severe that he volunteered for service in Afghanistan to escape the Center of Excellence. We've got a very severe problem.

Mr. LYNCH. Okay. I don't have any more time to delve into it, but, again, I appreciate the testimony of all the witnesses. Thanks for your help.

Mr. FARENTHOLD. Thank you very much.

We'll now recognize the vice chairman of the subcommittee, Mr. Walberg.

Mr. WALBERG. Thank you, Mr. Chairman. And thank you to the witnesses for taking additional stance in difficult circumstances.

Dr. Van Boven, if you would, please describe the nature of the public health threat to the veterans from traumatic brain injury.

Dr. VAN BOVEN. Well, I think the more you look, the more you find. You know, years ago, something like this had another name, it was called shell shock and you get over it. And, in fact, Eric Hipple, who I speak with, the former Detroit Lion and sports concussion expert, spoke in terms of, well, there's a badge of honor to see the stars.

Mr. WALBERG. I sat on the plane with him yesterday coming here, so.

Dr. VAN BOVEN. Fantastic. Exactly. Well, you're why he didn't have dinner with me. Just kidding.

Mr. WALBERG. Sorry about that.

Dr. VAN BOVEN. No, no. He's a great guy. But the point is, he's a spokesperson on the issue, and the issue is that it's a cumulative effect. It's like radiation. We're learning that multiple concussions, they build up and they can have additive effect. The same nodes or circuits that are messed up can set the stage to increase your risk of post-traumatic stress disorder, chronic traumatic encephalopathy, and be victims like Muhammad Ali. We are now, like, saying, wait a minute, this is a disaster. We've got to work on this and we've got to get serious, because if you don't look, you won't find.

Mr. WALBERG. How many vets has it struck?

Dr. VAN BOVEN. Well, the veterans, gosh, almighty, I think that that is something that we haven't scratched on. Look, in 2005, just in soldiers, we said, oh, maybe there's about 2,700; 2007, maybe 4,000; by 2008, we said, well, maybe there's 150,000; and now we've decided there's 300,000. So it's a matter of sensitivity.

Now, veterans, my goodness, it's almost, I think it's going to take the same amount of time it took to recognize Agent Orange. Now, there are a lot of confounds because guess what makes TBI worse? Alcohol, substance abuse, sleep deprivation, stressors. It's a toxic mix.

And so it's no wonder, and I say this really tragically, that so many of our veterans of war end up spiraling down socially and economically. They lose their wife, they lose their life, and they end up plummeting down to the VA system, which takes the bottom 20 percent or less economically that give health care. There's these million vets, for example, that the VA takes care of.

I think that the problem is, when there's all these Federal employees, I think we need to help them by helping the people that are taking care of them so that when they see a problem they don't fear retribution, it, in fact, might be a badge of honor rather than denigration to be a whistleblower.

And then when you've got OSC, it reminds me of Eliot Ness, Eliot Ness trying to take on the mob. Look, with 120 people taking thousands and thousands of claims with a $2.5 million budget, how can you expect them to do their job?

Mr. WALBERG. So concluding that research and continued research and consistent research is necessary, with respect to the funds for TBI research, where did the money go?

Dr. VAN BOVEN. There were ghost employees, people that didn't set foot in a lab, but they were taken from payroll. There was no accounting. There was no budgeting.

Mr. WALBERG. And it was used for what?

Dr. VAN BOVEN. Well, it was used for people that were on salary but not doing research. It was used for scanner time that was frivolously used for, I'm sorry, some kind of experimentation. I mean, I couldn't understand it. So I sent it off to five reviewers across the Nation to kind of make sense of something——

Mr. WALBERG. And you found out how many vets were being helped?

Dr. VAN BOVEN. Zero. Not one veteran was treated at the BIRL, and not one study has been done on veterans at Waco. Zero. Thirteen million dollars and 8, 9 years later.

Mr. WALBERG. What motive did the DVA have to cover up the funding diversion instead of ending it? I mean, in your mind. What motive?

Dr. VAN BOVEN. I don't know what that stands. I'm sorry. Oh, yes, sorry. Thank you. It's got a new name. He was asking about JCAHO. But it's now called the Joint Commission. That's why I was confused.

So the motivation is very simple, and Ed Sherwood testified to it. He said, I am getting ready because we are in the bottom 10 percent of the Joint Commission for clinical performance—and this is all testimony, I am paraphrasing—and he said, and, you know, the director is getting a lot of heat over it. And he told me, he said, you know, I could lose my job because of this. He said, so before JCAHO comes in and tears us apart and we lose our job and get zapped by them—I am quoting, I am paraphrasing—he said, I get my friend, this administrator, to get in there and clean things up to keep the hospital accredited, and in turn I give him research dollars, although he hadn't done any published work, any reports, any progress, no science. It didn't matter because this was just basically money that he had power of, he wasn't a scientist, but he could just use it to help protect his job. That was the motive.

Mr. WALBERG. Mr. Chairman, could I follow up or am I out of time?

Mr. FARENTHOLD. Without objection, we will give you another minute.

Mr. WALBERG. Thank you. Thank you. That may be all it needs. Did this coverup serve or obstruct WPA's efforts, their goals?

Dr. VAN BOVEN. I think it was in a vacuum. I don't think WPA was anywhere in anyone's mind. And any time I would raise prohibited personnel practices I was admonished and chastised during these internal tribunals, saying we are not here to hear about this, these kind of what you think are illicit motives of retaliatory animus, we are here to talk about you, Dr. Van Boven. And so it was completely cut out.

Mr. WALBERG. And the peer review process didn't work?

Dr. VAN BOVEN. Well, the peer review, if I may, you know, part of the problem, you saw the chief of staff who reigned over his own grievance against him and found himself not guilty. I think that that's symbolic and representative of the VA system right now.

Look, we have an office inspector general, an Office of Research Oversight who is supposed to investigate his boss, the VA, and then but also answer to his boss. I mean that's where you get all this incredibly diluted type of reports from ORO and the OIG. I think we need outside independent assessments. Health care is the same problem.

Look, I am sorry I've got to inject this. Because I am a neurologist. I take care of patients. In 1999, the Institute of Medicine reported that ''To Err is Human,'' that there was 100,000 people dying in hospitals every year from medical mistakes. Okay? And so Congress was really up in arms, and we are going to do something, and we are going to improve transparency in government. Right? Fifteen years later, the Leapfrog organization this fall has reported that that number of hospital errors causing deaths has quadrupled,

400,000 a year. It is the number three killer of Americans now behind heart attack and cancer.

If you go to the Joint Commission and speak to Hal Bressler, who is the chief counsel there, who has been there for 30 years—again, entrenched bureaucrat—and you ask him about, hey, I got some disclosures of problems, because you know, who knows but the doctors in the trenches, patients don't understand the details, and they shouldn't have to, but when doctors feel so much fear they can't speak out, well, guess what happens? Hal Bressler of the Joint Commission said, Robert, to my lawyers, very simple, he said the problem is there has only been two cases ever, of even though it's on the books that hospitals cannot retaliate for whistleblowing or, you know, sharing sentinel events that cause a patient's death, although it's against the law and against our policies, there is no protections. We can't do subpoenas. We can't do investigations. Therefore, unless the hospital is stupid enough—and there were two cases in history—to say, yeah, we did it, we committed the murder, and punished him for reporting to you, unless they do that, Joint Commission can't do anything.

We need laws. Think about it. You know those reports about you can save lives every year, thousands of them, thousands every year, guaranteed, if you provide protection and support for physicians in hospitals.

Mr. WALBERG. Thank you.

And thank you, Mr. Chairman.

Mr. FARENTHOLD. Thank you very much.

We will now recognize the ranking member of the full committee for his questioning.

Mr. CUMMINGS. Thank you very much, Mr. Chairman.

I want to say to all of you, I agree with Mr. Lynch, your testimony has been extremely helpful. And I think there is no member of the committee and the Congress that fails to feel strongly about protecting whistleblowers. It is very, very important.

And, Ms. Lerner, as I listened to you, I think we are having some success. I think that is why you are seeing as much action as you are seeing, and that's a good thing.

One of the reforms included in the landmark Whistleblower Protection Enhancement Act is a 2-year pilot program that allows whistleblowers to appeal a judgment of the Merit Systems Protection Board to any U.S. court of appeals with jurisdiction. Prior to the establishment of the pilot program, the Federal Circuit was the only court of appeals with authority to adjudicate whistleblower appeals.

Mr. Devine, I understand that prior to the creation of the pilot program the track record for decisions in the Federal circuit was adverse to whistleblowers. I think it was something like 3 to 226 against whistleblowers for decisions on the merits. Is that right?

Mr. DEVINE. It degenerated to 3 in 232.

Mr. CUMMINGS. Oh, okay. Can you explain for us the concern that the pilot program was meant to address?

Mr. DEVINE. Yes, sir. It was meant to create healthy competition, to translate the terms of the act when there was dispute about them, the same as we rely on in every other aspect of the legal system, having a difference of opinions and finding the truth from the composite.

It's needed even more. The Federal circuit has not ruled in favor of a whistleblower on the merits since passage of the WPEA. They have not been born again. And in the meantime, other courts of appeals have been coming in. And in fact on whether the rights were retroactive, one court of appeals said we don't need to determine that because the Federal circuit rulings all along were erroneous, and we are going to, by the court opinion, restore all the rights that the Federal circuit took away.

If we had had all circuits review, we wouldn't have had to keep passing the Whistleblower Protection Act over and over again, because the aberration of one hostile court would have been subsumed.

We are very grateful that the House has passed legislation extending the 2-year pilot test to 5 years, because the GAO study to see whether it worked or not is 4 years, and we hope that the Senate follows suit on that.

I'd also like to supplement the answer on peer review as not being part of the solution at the DVA. It actually was the primary vehicle to attack the whistleblowers at the DVA. It's the classic star chamber proceeding in that they are not allowed to know the charges against them, they are not allowed to see the witnesses testifying against them, they are not allowed to present their own witnesses. It was a vehicle to be able to give an undefended, unreviewable attack on the whistleblower. And the same solution for retaliatory criminal investigations, if applied to retaliatory peer reviews, the same upgrade of language from legislative history culled from the 1994 amendments would allow people like Dr. Van Boven to defend himself before he has to go to the MSPB for a hearing.

Mr. CUMMINGS. Chairman Grundmann, what impact has the all-circuit review provisions of the Whistleblower Protection Enhancement Act had on the Board's adjudication of whistleblower cases?

Ms. GRUNDMANN. In short, not much. There have only been four cases appealed outside the circuit. And of the four cases, only two of them have been decided. The other two are still pending. So as Mr. Devine indicated, if the goal of this law is to develop a wide variety of decisions from different circuits, then I would suggest that four decisions is not many.

Mr. CUMMINGS. At the time this provision was considered in the Protection Act there was a concern that allowing for whistleblower appeals to other circuit courts of appeal would result in a flood of cases being filed in the other courts. My last question, Chairman Grundmann, can you tell us how many cases have been filed in other circuits?

Ms. GRUNDMANN. Just four.

Mr. CUMMINGS. Four?

Ms. GRUNDMANN. Four total, on one hand.

Mr. CUMMINGS. And does that surprise you?

Ms. GRUNDMANN. That's a difficult question to answer, because it does take a while for a case to complete itself, complete its process, and then be filed in court. But we've been tracking this for 2 years, and all we've seen is four cases in total.

Mr. CUMMINGS. So, Mr. Devine, you said you'd like to see that legislation extended, the pilot program extended another 3 years?

Mr. DEVINE. Yes, sir.

Mr. CUMMINGS. Consistent with what we passed.

Mr. DEVINE. Very supportive of the bill the House passed to make it 5 years.

Mr. CUMMINGS. And do you think that will make a difference? It sounds like it is almost a little early to even make a good judgment on it based on what you said and what Chairwoman Grundmann said.

Mr. DEVINE. Yes, sir. Well, we would love to see this made permanent as far as having a research base to demonstrate that. It's going to take more than a few years to develop an adequate number of cases for a statistically significant base.

Mr. CUMMINGS. Thank you very much, Mr. Chairman.

Mr. FARENTHOLD. Thank you very much.

We will now recognize the chairman of the full committee, the gentleman from southern California, Mr. Issa.

Mr. ISSA. Thank you, Mr. Chairman. This is one of those bipartisan things that brings together both sides of the dais, and so I'll follow up where the ranking member left off.

Mr. Devine, if I hear you are right, and if I look at what I think Mr. Cummings noted, and, Ms. Grundmann, you said, which is there is no flood. So it is a relatively small amount of cases. And if we extend—and I appreciate the comment about making it permanent—but if we extend it significantly we do no harm, that the original short period of time was based on the assumption that there might be a flood and we might have it look at it. Is that pretty much the consensus of everybody there?

Mr. DEVINE. Yes, sir. The predictions of a flood of cases either for normal access to appeals courts or for jury trials in district court have always flunked the reality test. They have been challenged prior to the passage of a dozen laws for corporate whistleblowers at the district court level, for example. That flood has simply never occurred. It has been crying wolf over and over and over.

Ms. GRUNDMANN. Let me just add briefly——

Mr. ISSA. Yes, please.

Ms. GRUNDMANN. —as I am obligated to do, that is a policy call for Congress. We don't take a position on it. But as I stated, the statistics do not provide much of a basis for anybody to draw any conclusions at this point.

Mr. ISSA. So without taking a position, the numbers speak for themselves that there isn't a flood. And if we are going to evaluate the benefits and, to be honest, to see some of these cases come to maturity, it may take more time than was originally planned in the pilot.

Ms. GRUNDMANN. That is correct.

Mr. ISSA. Thank you.

Mr. MacLean, I want to thank you for the work that you have done to further, if you will, our awareness. The fact is that I look forward to your case being fully adjudicated. And I think in fact that's part of what we on the dais want to make sure is made available, is access to whistleblowers in an appropriate venue of their choosing, and then let's see ultimately when they trickle up to the Supreme Court how they are decided.

Ms. Lerner, you have been a tremendous champion, and I appreciate the work that you have done. And this is a subcommittee hearing and I know that before I got in here from other duties most of this was done, but I want to take a moment and thank you for being, if you will, a good public servant.

And, quite frankly, for all of you, this hearing is about an area in which this committee is passionate. There is very little time left in this Congress. But if we can in fact do a further draft, the ranking member and myself, and get it introduced in the lame duck, we will. And that will take a little time.

But this hearing today, Mr. Chairman, does help us. So with that, I yield back.

Mr. FARENTHOLD. Thank you very much, Mr. Chairman.

We will now recognize the gentlelady from the District of Columbia.

Ms. NORTON. Thank you, Mr. Chairman. I am very pleased that we are having this hearing. And I am pleased that the chairman is here because this, the bipartisan Whistleblower Protection Enhancement Act, I think is an indication of the concern of Congress, continuing concern I must say. Indeed, as I listened to Ms. Grundmann speak of having sat in my class on negotiations, I can only think that she has accomplished a lot more than any negotiations class could have given her, as she has risen to become chair of the Merit Systems Protection Board.

Ms. Grundmann, I retain my tenure at Georgetown. I teach a seminar called Lawmaking and Statutory Interpretation. It's interesting that as long as they are writing about statutory interpretation and how it mixes or links with what we pass, they can write on any subject they want to. And I note that I have learned something about your decisions and the decisions of the Federal circuit, because any number of them over the years have chosen to write on what looks to be the conflict between the statute and what the Board and the Federal circuit have found.

And then I note that Congress has kept trying to revise this statute. And I don't know if we need to try again, listening to some of the other ways to approach it that have come out in this hearing.

I want to raise another issue that could affect far more Federal employees, conceivably virtually every Federal employee, and wipe out altogether the Whistleblower Enhancement Act. And I am referring to Kaplan v. Conyers, a decision that reversed what the Merit Systems Protection Board found in favor of the Federal employees. And the administration appealed all the way to the Federal circuit and the Supreme Court. And the Supreme Court has let that stand.

We use the word security very loosely. This is a frightening circumstance, where an agency head or his designee can designate any position as security sensitive. Understand these are not positions that require a security clearance. So in the parlance of the day, most people would not understand that these positions are commonplace positions, having nothing to do with security. And I want to ask the chairman if I could enter into the record the statements of two of the organizations that represent the Federal employees on the impact of this decision.

Mr. FARENTHOLD. Without objection, so ordered.

Ms. NORTON. The first thing I thought about when I looked at this decision was the Whistleblower Protection Act means nothing because there is no appeal whatsoever. It seems to me to go against everything that Congress has passed for the last 50 years. So if you think that you're a victim of retaliation or that somebody has discriminated against you because of your religion or your race, leave alone trying to retaliate against you, there is nothing you can say because there is no recourse.

So I have to say, is there any civil service system? And why isn't that an incentive for agency heads to simply disregard the system altogether?

Now, I am pleased to note that I have introduced a bill, and there are two Republicans and three Democrats in this committee who have sponsored this bill, and the Senate has adopted this bill, and it is a bipartisan bill now in the Senate. So you can see that this troubles the Congress itself.

How to deal with a new wrinkle, I would call it, a new layer, first time I have ever heard of a layer, outside of security. So by calling these security-sensitive positions, these positions have been tucked right in there with positions where you need a security clearance. And you can understand where there is a security clearance and the kinds of information that could not in fact come forward. These are not those positions.

And I want to ask about the impact of the Conyers ruling, particularly on our attempts to protect whistleblowers, and for that matter on Federal employees across the country—across the board—recognizing that these first cases have involved DOD employees. But I read nothing in the regulations that would, even though most DOD employees of course do not have security clearance, but I read nothing in the regulations that even confine it to DOD employees. And I note that the administration is trying to expand with further regulations the position it has taken by apparently writing regulations as I speak by the OPM and the office of national intelligence that would expand the Federal positions labeled by this new label, security sensitive, to virtually all Federal employees.

I would like to hear, especially I would like to what all of you think. I suppose I should begin with Ms. Lerner, the Special Counsel, and see if she has any role in advising the administration, which is I think taking the Conyers decision and raising it to even further levels that are unheard of in what has been called up until this point a civil service system.

Ms. LERNER. Thank you for your question.

Up until now, we have not had a role in advising the administration on this issue. I think it is important to note, however, that Congress has set up the Office of Special Counsel as a safe channel for disclosing classified information. So there is no doubt about the Office of Special Counsel's ability to responsibly and appropriately handle these cases. I don't know that that has been mentioned or acknowledged. And I know you have introduced legislation, and as you mentioned the Senate has, too. But that's something to keep in mind in response to any objections to employees having the ability to appeal to the Office of Special Counsel.

Ms. NORTON. Are you saying even secure positions?

Ms. LERNER. Yes. Yeah. We can handle classified information and secure positions.

Ms. NORTON. Mr. Devine, do you think a legislative remedy is necessary? And I should ask Ms. Grundmann, inasmuch as the Merit Systems Protection Board ruled in favor of the employees and was overruled in the Federal circuit. Do you think legislation, whether the legislation I introduced or has been introduced in the Senate or other legislation, could in fact correct this situation?

Ms. GRUNDMANN. That is what I understand to be the goal of the legislation you introduced. But again, we have no position on policy. However, I can say that we have argued before the Federal circuit precisely the types of statements and arguments that you have made here today, which is there would be no way for us or any third party to know whether somebody was removed for an improper reason such as whistleblowing or retaliation for whistleblowing.

Right now, because of the state of the law, we are bound to follow the Conyers, Northover decision, which precludes our review in its entirety. Let me also note that there are certain agencies out there that have only noncritical sensitive positions. Everybody has some sort of sensitivity designation. So all the individuals potentially in that agency don't have any MSPB review.

Ms. NORTON. DOD and others as well?

Ms. GRUNDMANN. There are components within the Department of Defense. I think the labor unions, the statements that you submitted you will find those comments. In the two particular cases that appeared before the Board, both these individuals were low-graded individuals. They are low-level GS employees who did not have access to classified information. In fact, their ineligibility was based on determinations, personal determinations, mostly financial, credit rating, bankruptcies.

Ms. NORTON. Mr. Devine, just finally could you say something on a legislative solution here? Or am I overwrought about what this does to the Whistleblower Protection Act or, for that matter, to Federal employees more generally?

Mr. DEVINE. To my great dismay, no, you are not overwrought. I have been working on good government rights through Federal employees making a contribution since 1976, and this is the most severe threat that's occurred. Whistleblower rights were immediately a target of the Conyers lawsuit thanks to the White House decision. But trying to build whistleblower rights without a foundation of the merit system is trying to build a home without a foundation. And when the security clearance precedent took away access to the civil service system and the MSPB, it was only a matter of time before whistleblower protection rights were next. It was inevitable. It happened.

And there is not any question in our mind that the days are numbered for the Whistleblower Protection Act's survival if this decision is not reversed. I wish that it weren't necessary to have legislation, because having worked four times to pass the Whistleblower Protection Act we know how hard that is and how long it takes and how much work it is. But there isn't any other option left.

And it shouldn't be controversial legislation. It's just to restore the status quo for a merit system and Federal employment that existed from 1883 to 2013 without any incident due to the lack of sensitive job designations. This should not be a controversial bill.

And there is no time to waste. Agencies, at the Department of State, agency by agency, they are starting to make all their employees sensitive, noncritical sensitive. All the IGs that we depend on to protect the whistleblowers are transforming their employees to be critical sensitive. The entire Border Patrol, where we have had some of the most significant whistleblowing disclosures, will all be noncritical sensitive. The government is being transformed from the rule of law to a national security spoils system.

Ms. NORTON. Thank you, Mr. Chairman. I don't know if the administration knows what it is doing, but it is wiping out the civil service system, it seems to me.

Mr. FARENTHOLD. I thank you for your line of questioning. And I actually do want to follow up on it. I mean, I think we do have an issue of sensitivity creep. And I think Mr. Lynch pointed out our challenges in drafting legislation that is appropriate for that. I mean, I think clearly the case of someone stocking sunglasses is not going to have access to sensitive information, but I think the majority of us would agree that Mr. Snowden clearly had access to and exposed sensitive information.

So finding the right place to draw the line is challenging. I know it's certainly something that's going to be critical to Mr. MacLean in his ongoing litigation as to how that goes. Anything we do now probably won't help you. You are in the courts' hands.

But I would appreciate, and you don't have to come up from it now, I'd actually request that if you all in the next few days could send to the committee any thoughts you would have on how we draft that language to protect the legitimate whistleblower while still protecting our national security interests. And a piece of it may be where that information is released. Clearly flying overseas and releasing NSA information, as Mr. Snowden did, is not appropriate. But coming to a congressional committee, or a special counsel, or the Office of Inspector General with your agency might be an appropriate place to do that. And as we look at reworking that, at least I would appreciate each of you all's thoughts and input on how to do that.

I do have a couple of questions that I want to hit. Mr. Devine, you offered your five concerns, your five loopholes, if you will, that you think need addressing. And I would like to ask our other witnesses—I realize Ms. Lerner and Ms. Grundmann, as government employees you are kind of in an awkward situation there. I would ask that if you feel comfortable speaking for yourself rather than the agency, someone with knowledge in the field, you're welcome to answer. I'll understand if you decline to answer.

But if any of you all have any other suggestions for improvements in the law overall, I would like to hear. I am giving you an out, Ms. Lerner, but we will start with you.

Ms. LERNER. I think it's an important question. I would like to be able to give it some thought.

Mr. FARENTHOLD. Okay. Send it on with your thoughts on the language on the sensitivity creep, as we will call it.

Ms. LERNER. Sure.

Mr. FARENTHOLD. And Ms. Grundmann?

Ms. GRUNDMANN. Well, in terms of that particular issue, the Board has already spoken through its decision. I think we were rather clear on how we felt the issue should be handled. The Federal circuit disagreed with us. So certainly it is in this body's hands to resolve any outstanding issues. We will follow up with you, however.

Mr. FARENTHOLD. Mr. MacLean?

Mr. MACLEAN. Throughout my case, the TSA just thumbed its nose at MSPB orders and Federal circuit court orders. So the agencies are allowed to get away with what they do because I think the MSPB is too weak to uphold the orders. And they just go ahead and ignore them, such as switching out witnesses and ignoring deposition orders.

Mr. FARENTHOLD. So some teeth in dealing with folks within agencies who disregard the whistleblower protection might be something you would suggest? I don't want to put words in your mouth.

Mr. MACLEAN. It's hard to say, because there was just never any accountability when the final decisions came from the full Board. And I think they are overwhelmed with a lot of caseload. It's good that this is opened up to multiple circuits, because I think the Federal circuit was overloaded with this. And now it's good that it's been spread around. So now they can spend more time to take a look at this.

Mr. FARENTHOLD. Dr. Van Boven, you have any thoughts?

Dr. VAN BOVEN. Well, with regards to where to draw the line——

Mr. FARENTHOLD. Can you turn your microphone on? Why am I the only one you all forget to turn your microphones on with?

Dr. VAN BOVEN. I am sorry. I don't have the expertise to comment on where to draw the line on sensitivity issues and whistleblowers' rights. But with regards to more broader suggestions on my plight and history and what are lessons learned and how can we improve that, I have the following suggestions.

Number one, I think that there should be outside, independent investigations with regards to wrongdoing in an agency. I think it's a conflict of interest when you have to have the, as I mentioned before, a chief of staff who is making a decision and deciding about whether or not he did something wrong. So, too, I think that there needs to be agencies that can have independent assessment. Oh, that's the OSC.

So my feeling is that OIGs and the OROs and all the rest, it is a comedy of errors. I think that you should put teeth into OSC, 120 people, $2.5 million. I'm sorry, she didn't pay me for this, but I think that if you really want to do it, then give them the guns and the power to help people.

And the second thing is we need more cultural top-down saying it is not the whistleblower that has the problem. He is blowing the whistle because something is wrong, and we need to try to 'fess up and give incentives. Either the stick, just like in hospitals, you have a patient that is staying too long and they come back 3 days after you discharge them and they die, well, gosh, there's penalties there. And then also the carrot in terms of we are going to have rewards for people who show real improvements in performances. And I always say to my patients it is better to prick your own bubble than have someone else prick it for you. So I am my own toughest critic in terms of so they have rewards for those that point out problems in themselves before someone blows the whistle.

Mr. FARENTHOLD. Thank you very much. Listen, I couldn't agree with you more about needing to get to the bottom of some of the cultural problem. And again, I don't intend to beat up on the VA, but they seem to have asked for it. And hopefully we have been able to do that with our recent legislation.

Finally, I want to wrap my questioning up—and we will give Mr. Lynch a second round of questioning when I am done—with a broad overview. Each one of you is involved directly with whistleblowers. Some of you are whistleblowers yourselves. This committee relies heavily on whistleblowers. Quite frankly, the American people rely heavily on whistleblowers. It's the people who have the courage to do the right thing and point out what's going wrong, sometimes at their own peril. We're trying to fix it where it isn't as perilous for them. But these are true American heroes who do the right thing and come forward.

I want to give each one of you the opportunity, whoever is watching this on the Web that might be thinking about being a whistleblower, or somebody who is reading the transcript of this hearing that's thinking about being a whistleblower, take 10 or 15 or 30 seconds, what would you say to somebody who is thinking about becoming a whistleblower? We'll go down the line and start with Ms. Lerner. And when we are done I will pass on to Mr. Lynch.

Ms. LERNER. I think what I would say to a whistleblower is that they have a lot of avenues to come forward. And I particularly want them to think about the Office of Special Counsel. We are a robust, active agency. We are understaffed, but we are getting terrific results for whistleblowers. We have a record number of corrective actions, almost 200 this year, on behalf of whistleblowers.

We need people to come forward with their disclosures. And I think the results that we have gotten, because whistleblowers have come to us, show the value. We have gotten amazing results at the Air Force, the FAA, the Department of Homeland Security, and most recently at the VA.

And just today in fact the new Secretary of the VA I believe testified that he wanted everybody to be a whistleblower at the VA. Probably going a little bit too far. But the message is I think he wants people to know that the culture is going to change at the VA. And we need whistleblowers to come forward in order to make our agencies, our government better and safer for the American public.

Mr. FARENTHOLD. Ms. Grundmann.

Ms. GRUNDMANN. Thank you. One of our functions of course is a study function. And we have routinely seen that Federal employees still perceive evidence of prohibited personnel practices, one of them being reprisals for whistleblowing. So that creates a culture problem.

We commend this body for taking the initiative to change the law to create new avenues for whistleblowers to come forward. But ultimately, as Ranking Member Lynch mentioned at the beginning, the culture needs to change within an agency whereby employees are encouraged to come forward and whereby their allegations are investigated.

And when the investigation is done, if there is no wrongdoing accomplished, employees should be told an investigation was completed and you did the right thing by coming forward. So the culture change is what needs to occur, and it's educational and it's long term.

Mr. FARENTHOLD. Thank you very much.

Mr. MacLean.

Mr. MACLEAN. I would advise people that your whole life is going to change. It doesn't matter what you believed what was doing right at the time. Years down the road everything that you said and done is going to be highly scrutinized. A lot of your friends at work are never going to talk to you again. You could lose your job. It's a huge, huge risk. Prepare for the absolute worst.

Mr. FARENTHOLD. Would you do it again?

Mr. MACLEAN. Absolutely. I was a law enforcement officer. You paid me three times, four times more than your average Federal worker to make split decisions in one of the most dangerous areas to enforce the law. So it was my duty. It was my oath to do what I had to do. And at the time, I believed I was doing everything to protect the public.

So absolutely. I took that law enforcement oath. So I would do it again and again. Better people than me have given up worse, given up more.

Mr. FARENTHOLD. Thank you very much.

Dr. Van Boven.

Dr. VAN BOVEN. Right now these are——

Mr. FARENTHOLD. Microphone.

Dr. VAN BOVEN. I'm sorry. Right now, I think that the applause for whistleblowing is frustratingly anemic at best. I think that the current culture is that you have to be masochistic, a Don Quixote, or want to have financial ruin and have a Pyrrhic victory and a probable divorce. And these are the statistics.

Look at Lois Jenson of the first class action lawsuit in America. I lived a few miles from where she was up in, Virginia, Minnesota. After 12 years, she and a half dozen people got $600,000, but her life was ruined, and she is still a wreck. If we think in terms of Mr. Wigand of the tobacco industry, he has been psychologically devastated as a result of all these things. I myself, thankfully, I survived, but barely.

So the bottom line is you know we got Boy Scouts and Girl Scouts, you give them badges. We should start early and really make it happen. Where is my badge? I think that if we really want to give positive reinforcements, then make it visible and to say you are a hero and mean it. Because right now people say, oh, they want to applaud a whistleblower, but they don't want to be too close to the whistle.

Mr. FARENTHOLD. Thank you very much.

And, Mr. Devine.

Mr. DEVINE. Mr. Chairman, the first thing I would say is that this is unsurpassed as a crossroads decision in your life, which will never be the same. Make this decision with your family and the loved ones who are depending on you, because they are going to be affected by it. And the cost will be severe if you are going to make a significant difference.

But if you are willing to pay the price, you can make a difference, because there is nothing more powerful than the truth. So think it over.

Number two, do your homework. It's the highest risk decision you will be making, and you have to do the most advanced preparation. So get that book, "The Whistleblower's Survival Guide: A Handbook for Committing the Truth." It's based on the experience of 6,000 whistleblowers' lessons learned.

And the third thing I'd advise, if they're a Federal civil servant, to convince Congress to give you rights that are analogous to those of corporate employees who have full, normal access to court to enforce them.

Mr. FARENTHOLD. Thank you very much.

Mr. Lynch.

Mr. LYNCH. Thank you.

Normally, I would say the witnesses have suffered enough, but I do have a couple other questions. Just as sort of an anecdote, in Boston the VA has switched over. They have done this whole whistleblower support protocol. I was just involved in a case at one of my local VA hospitals—I have got three—where the whistleblowers' complaints were borne out and the system was changed because they came forward. It's not entirely a happy ending, but I have to say that they came forward, they pointed out deficiencies, and those deficiencies were changed. Somewhat reluctantly, but they were changed.

So there is the opportunity, I think, to educate our folks, our managers, to implement these programs to make it more conducive for people to come forward. And I think that part we need to do better and we need to do it all across government. And I think that will help change the culture in a way if we are seen as supporting this, and maybe by that way, by that action, the risk that Mr. MacLean talked about.

And I hate hearing that, that you take your life in your hands. And maybe we haven't really drilled down on Mr. MacLean's case, but I will do that now. You served as an air marshal back in 2003. And what I understand is in August 2003 TSA proposed a change in policy to cancel all air marshal coverage on long distance flights for that time period. And it coincided with a period of high risk on the airlines, long distance airlines, from Al Qaeda. Isn't that correct?

Mr. MACLEAN. Yes, sir.

Mr. LYNCH. And you came forward after you received your notice, which was nonclassified at the time, and you complained about it. And you also, as you described earlier in your testimony, you went to the press, and they confirmed it with other air marshals. And instead of being rewarded for your diligence—of course TSA had to change their policy—you were fired in what, 2006?

Mr. MACLEAN. Yes, sir.

Mr. LYNCH. And the excuse they used was that they had gone retroactively and in 2006 changed their classification of your text messages that you received to classified. And so you were in a sensitive position. Is that what their argument is basically?

Mr. MacLean. They retroactively designated my disclosure with an agency-regulated unclassified marking called sensitive security information years after the fact.

Mr. Lynch. Right. And so you were fired for that.

Mr. MacLean. Yes, sir.

Mr. Lynch. Tell me and tell this committee about the difficulty you have had in getting employment as an air marshal or other employment since that job action.

Mr. MacLean. I applied for almost a dozen police agencies in southern California, and none of them even came forward and said we don't want to hire you because you got fired from the TSA. I simply got, thanks for applying, you weren't the most qualified, maybe try again in the future.

I only had a high school diploma, didn't have a college degree. So it was very difficult for me. And most of the jobs, I have been jumping job to job with commission only, door-to-door sales jobs. It's about the only thing I could find.

So, yeah, I was pretty much blackballed, being a veteran, Air Force veteran, a Border Patrol agent. The man who fired me said I had an impeccable, perfect record. It didn't matter. I still couldn't get a job as a cop again.

Mr. Lynch. What exactly were you told about how your career may be harmed if you didn't remain silent? Were there any warnings given to you about what you were doing coming forward?

Mr. MacLean. After the fourth proper channel that I went through, which was finally a special agent with the inspector general, he simply said the agency went broke. This happens. There is nothing you can do, there is nothing we can do, you don't want to cut your career short over making a big deal about this. And that was the final time, I was advised not to go further.

Mr. Lynch. Well, I think the circumstances that you find yourself in is a disgrace to us as Federal employers, both yourself and Dr. Van Boven. And I think your example is extremely instructive to us going forward in trying to devise a policy where employees like yourself will be protected during this process. I think you prevented a dangerous situation from being put upon the public, the flying public, and it's a disgrace that you're being punished for that.

So thank you for your testimony. As I said, I just wanted to spend a little time on your case and amplify it a little bit. Hopefully, it will help you going forward.

Mr. MacLean. Thank you, sir.

Mr. Lynch. Thank you.

Mr. Farenthold. I'd like to thank everybody on our witness, especially our whistleblowers. I'm going to echo what Mr. Lynch said, that it is a disgrace. And I hope you take away from this the members of this subcommittee I think unanimously are committed to making the situation better. And we are going to keep working on it. Again, thank you all for your testimony.

The subcommittee stands adjourned.

[Whereupon, at 3:45 p.m., the committee was adjourned.]

APPENDIX

MATERIAL SUBMITTED FOR THE HEARING RECORD

STATEMENT FOR THE RECORD

BY

COLLEEN M. KELLEY, NATIONAL PRESIDENT

NATIONAL TREASURY EMPLOYEES UNION

ON

EXAMINING THE ADMINISTRATION'S TREATMENT OF WHISTLEBLOWERS

BEFORE THE

SUBCOMMITTEE ON FEDERAL WORKFORCE, US POSTAL SERVICE AND THE CENSUS

HOUSE OVERSIGHT AND GOVERNMENT REFORM COMMITTEE

SEPTEMBER 9, 2014

Chairman Farenthold and Ranking Member Lynch: Thank you for giving the National Treasury Employees Union the opportunity to weigh in on one of the most important issues facing not just whistleblowers in the government, but a much larger segment of the federal workforce as well. As National President of NTEU, I represent over 150,000 employees in 31 agencies across government. Many of my members are in positions deemed "sensitive" by their agencies, and we are greatly concerned about the process used to make that designation and by the recent court ruling that threatens any review of agency decisions concerning the eligibility of employees to occupy "sensitive" positions. I am writing to ask this subcommittee's help in passing HR 3278, introduced by Rep. Norton, which will amend chapter 77 of title 5 to clarify certain due process rights of federal employees serving in "sensitive" positions.

HR. 3278 is necessary because in August 2013, the U. S. Court of Appeals for the Federal Circuit released its decision in Kaplan v. Conyers. In March 2014, the Supreme Court denied a request to review the Federal Circuit decision. The Federal Circuit Court ruled that the Merit Systems Protection Board (MSPB) could not engage in substantive review of Department of Defense (DoD) decisions concerning the eligibility of employees to occupy "sensitive" positions, even though the MSPB had been capably doing so for decades. While the decision was technically limited to DoD, its broad reasoning will almost certainly be extended to all agencies.

The ruling greatly expanded an earlier case (Egan) that held that the MSPB could not review agency security clearance determinations. We are not objecting to the Egan ruling. The positions at issue in Conyers and in HR 3278, do not involve security clearances or access to classified information.

The executive branch currently has unlimited discretion to designate positions as "sensitive". There is no monitoring or reporting of how agencies arrive at this decision and each agency can create its own guidelines. Indeed, there appears to be a great deal of inconsistency in how the determinations are made. In recent years, many agencies have designated huge numbers of employees as "sensitive". At Customs and Border Protection, for example, almost all of the roughly 24,000 bargaining unit positions represented by NTEU have been designated as "noncritical-sensitive", but only a small fraction require security clearances.

By allowing agencies to take unreviewable adverse actions against occupants of "sensitive" positions on the basis of eligibility, the Conyers decision provides incentives for agencies to continue to expand the number of positions designated as "sensitive" and to use eligibility as the basis for adverse actions since neither is subject to review. Once an agency has designated an employee as "sensitive", it can then deem that employee ineligible for his or her job.

Under Conyers, the MSPB cannot review the agency's reason for deeming an employee ineligible for a sensitive position. Without any review or oversight of its basis, an agency is free to deem an employee ineligible for any reason that it chooses. Some bases might be tangentially related to security (financial debt, for example, which, in an agency's eyes, might make an employee susceptible to coercion), but, without neutral review, there is nothing to stop an agency from deeming an employee ineligible for any reason—even a reason based on incorrect or incomplete information. Ms. Conyers, the named defendant in the case, was deemed ineligible based on inaccurate information about financial debt (debt that was her husband's). Importantly, without any neutral review, there is nothing to stop an agency from representing that an employee is ineligible for security reasons, even though the actual reason for the determination of ineligible is something more nefarious—for example, a discriminatory motive or a personal dislike of an employee who is capably performing her duties. Whistleblowers are particularly at risk since those that would retaliate would also likely afford themselves of a process that is not reviewable.

The Civil Service Reform Act sets out narrow national security exemptions to the adverse action appeals processes included in the law. The court's decision in an earlier case (Egan) held that the MSPB could not review agency security clearance determinations. However, the positions at issue in Conyers do not involve security clearances or access to classified information. The Conyers decision creates an exemption that swallows the rule, leaving hundreds of thousands of employees with little practical ability to ensure that adverse actions taken against them are legally appropriate. In essence, the Conyers decision allows the executive branch to ignore the Civil Service Reform Act. If the MSPB is not able to review eligibility determinations, agencies can remove, suspend, or demote any employee they deem "ineligible" without ever having to justify the basis for their determination.

We believe that Congress must take the lead on this important issue, and Rep. Norton's legislation will correct the loss of MSPB review for thousands of federal employees. We believe the bill is a sensible solution that balances national security and due process interests. We urge you to schedule a mark-up of the bill at your earliest convenience. Thank you for the opportunity to provide these comments on this important topic.

STATEMENT BY

J. DAVID COX, SR.
NATIONAL PRESIDENT
AMERICAN FEDERATION OF GOVERNMENT EMPLOYEES, AFL-CIO

BEFORE THE

SUBCOMMITTEE ON FEDERAL WORKFORCE, U.S. POSTAL SERVICE AND THE CENSUS OF THE
THE COMMITTEE ON OVERSIGHT AN GOVERNMENT REFORM

ON

EXAMINING THE ADMINISTRATION'S TREATMENT OF WHISTLEBLOWERS

SEPTEMBER 9, 2014

American Federation of Government Employees, AFL-CIO
80 F Street, NW, Washington, D.C. 20001 ★ (202) 737-8700 ★ www.afge.org

Mr. Chairman, Ranking Member Lynch, and Members of the Subcommittee: My name is J. David Cox, Sr., and I am the National President of the American Federation of Government Employees, AFL-CIO (AFGE), representing over 670,000 federal workers. I submit this statement for the hearing entitled: "Examining the Administration's Treatment of Whistleblowers." In 2012 Congress passed the Whistleblower Protection Enhancement Act (Public Law No. 112-199), a law closing loopholes that made it almost impossible for federal workers to protect themselves against retaliation when they expose wrongdoing on the job. Two years after this important victory federal workers and advocates of good government are fighting a decision by the U.S. Court of Appeals for the Federal Circuit in *Kaplan v. Conyers* that strikes at the heart of the merit system that has been the foundation of federal civil service, including protections against whistleblower retaliation. Because the U.S. Supreme Court declined to review the Federal Circuit's decision in *Conyers*, Congress must pass H.R. 3278, introduced by Del. Eleanor Homes Norton (D-DC), and Rep. Frank Wolf (R-VA) and Rep Rob Wittman (R-VA) and its Senate counterpart, S. 1809, to ensure that federal workers maintain the fundamental right of due process before the Merit Systems Protection Board (MSPB).

The *Conyers* decision does not apply to federal workers who hold security clearances and have access to classified information. The decision eliminates the right of federal workers who do not have access to classified information or hold a security clearance to challenge decisions regarding their eligibility to occupy positions that are redesignated from non-critical non-sensitive to non-critical sensitive to the MSPB, even though the MSPB has reviewed eligibility issues for decades. If *Conyers* stands, there will be no neutral review of whether the agency found an employee ineligible to occupy a position for an invidious or illegal reason. In addition, recently proposed regulations provide the framework for agencies to designate almost any job in government as a "national security position" and as a result allow agencies exempt a large group of employees holding those positions MSPB review of the agencies' eligibility decisions.

The combination of the *Conyers* decision and the proposed regulations would essentially undermine Civil Service Reform Act (Public Law 95-454) (CSRA) protections for a large and growing number of federal employees. The CSRA represents the system of oversight and accountability put in place by Congress to strengthen the federal workforce since its enactment in 1978. Under the CSRA, the MSPB acts as a vigorous defender of the merit system in the federal workplace. The MSPB protects federal employees from arbitrary disciplinary actions, inappropriate favoritism, and coercion for partisan political purposes. For the past 35 years, federal employees have turned to the MSPB when agencies abuse their authority by arbitrary actions, whistleblower reprisals or other forms of prohibited discrimination. This is how the MSPB facilitates the efficient and effective administration of the federal government and why MSPB review remains one of the most important due process protections for federal employees.

Congress must act on H.R. 3278 and its Senate companion S. 1809. The legislation simply restores the balanced accountability Congress originally intended under the CSRA by